Legacies of the
St. Louis
World's Fair

A compilation of articles by Bert Minkin.

Produced by the

www.1904worldsfairsociety.org

Printed in the United States of America

First Printing 1998
Second Printing 2004

Library of Congress Cataloging-in-Publication Data
1904 World's Fair Society
Minkin, Bert

Legacies of the St. Louis World's Fair by Bert Minkin,
Produced by The 1904 World's Fair Society
www.1904worldsfairsociety.org

ISBN 1-891442-05-8

1. St. Louis, Missouri - History
2. History - St. Louis, Missouri

Library of Congress number: Pending

Edited and proofread by: Yvonne Suess, Msgr. Edward Eichor, Diane Rademacher, Gertrude Rademacher, Ron Schira, Max Storm, and Pat Villmer.

In 1904, St. Louis secured its place in history
when it hosted the grandest exposition the
world has ever seen.

The world was educated.

The world was entertained.

The 1904 World's Fair Society,
founded on April 30, 1986,
has proudly produced this book of articles
written by Bert Minkin. Mr. Minkin's attention
to detail and historic accuracy
make this book a joy to read.

We want you to be educated.

We want you to be entertained.

1904 - 2004
WORLD'S FAIR CENTENNIAL

www.1904worldsfairsociety.org

This book is dedicated to the
memory of Bert Minkin.
His love of storytelling …
through the written word
and the spoken word …
was his greatest gift
to his community.

Bert Minkin
1951-1996

❧ Table of Contents ❧

A Word About the Fair

Our current vocabularies contain the names of many personalities and products connected with the Fair. Ice cream cones were originally dubbed World's Fair Cornucopias. Dr. Pepper, named after a Waco, Texas pharmacist, also debuted there.

The Brown Shoe Company still sells childrens' shoes under the Buster Brown trademark. Buster, his sister Mary Jane, and his dog Tige, were comic strip characters created by Richard Fenton Outcault in 1902. Remember Mary Jane shoes for girls? Outcault ran his own booth at the Fair where he sold rights to use his characters as product advertisements to over 50 manufacturers. The C.M. Miller Candy Company still markets a peanut butter confection under the Mary Jane trademark.

· · · · · · · · · ·
Ice cream cones were originally dubbed World's Fair Conucopias.
· · · · · · · · · ·

President Theodore Roosevelt spoke at the Fair's dedication ceremonies on April 30, 1903, and returned for a two day visit in November 1904. Teddy bears still bear his name.

Did you know Geronimo lived in the Apache Village

THE cleansing property of water depends upon its softness—hard water only half does its work. The addition of BORAX to the bath not only makes the cleansing process thorough, but it leaves one with a delightful feeling of lightness and freshness and coolness. The marvelous virtues of BORAX is due to a very simple law—it SOFTENS water.

BORAX differs in purity and quality, like other things. The purest and best Borax is

20-MULE-TEAM

BRAND. For sale at all drug and grocery stores in ¼, ½ and 1-lb. packages.

The famous "AMERICAN GIRL" PICTURES FREE to purchasers of 20-MULE-TEAM BORAX. At stores or sent for POUND BOX TOP and 4c. in stamps.
PACIFIC COAST BORAX COMPANY
New York   Chicago
San Francisco

This advertisement for 20-Mule-Team appeared in the August 1904 issue of the World's Fair Bulletin. (The World's Fair Publishing Company. From the collection of Ron Schira.)

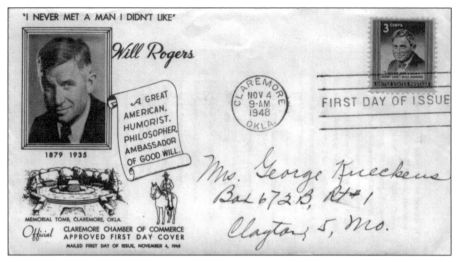

This commemorative envelope from 1948 was mailed on the "First Day of Issue" of the Will Rogers 3¢ stamp. Forty-four years after the Fair, and 13 years after his death, Will Rogers legacy was still in evidence. (From the collection of Ron Schira.)

on the fairgrounds from June 6 through October 2, 1904? This 75-year-old Apache tribal leader was part of the U.S. Department of the Interior's exhibit of Native American tribes. Souvenir hunters lined up to pay $2.00 for his autographed picture. An entire chapter of his memories is devoted to his St. Louis experiences. During World War II, U.S. Army Airborne paratroopers adopted his name as their battle cry. The 82nd Airborne claims to have started this tradition.

During the Fair, Geronimo and 24 year old Will Rogers performed in Colonel Zach Mullhall's Wild West Show at Delmar Gardens Race Track. Rogers' numerous contributions to the English language included his own epitaph, "I've joked about nearly every prominent man of my day, but I never met a man I didn't like."

After the St. Louis World's Fair closed on December 1, 1904, the Ferris Wheel, originally constructed for Chicago's 1893 Columbian Exposition, was dynamited. It was constructed by Dr. George Washington Gale Ferris. Local legend has it that parts of it were buried in Forest Park, but no documentation has been found to turn that legend into fact.

Guglielmo Marconi visited the Fair to demonstrate the wireless transmitter and receiver he invented in 1896. Radios were originally called Marconis. Marconigram was a registered trademark.

One of the Fair's most colorful characters was Borax Bill who drove his 20-mule team for Francis Marion Smith's Borax Soap Company. Borax and Boraxo are still on the market.

These Legacies of the St. Louis World's Fair are not the only legacies still in existence. Keep your eyes open as you travel through the city and the world, and see what other legacies you might find. ❖

This advertisement for Dr. Pepper appeared regularly in the World's Fair Bulletin. (The World's Fair Publishing Company. From the collection of Ron Schira.)

Remember Poor Louis

"Another Louis, Louis," composer Kerry Mills called out while sitting at a New York bar with song lyricist, Andrew B. Sterling, in 1904. Mills was ordering a refill of a popular alcoholic concoction then known as a Louis, from a familiar bartender named Louis.

Mills was ordering a refill of a popular alcoholic concoction.

Mills' chance repetition of Louis amused Sterling, and reminded him that the St. Louis World's Fair was scheduled to open on April 30, 1904. Sterling then decided to use the catchy name repetition in a timely song lyric promoting the Fair.

The lyricist whose roster of hits would eventually include, *Merrily We Roll Along, Wait Till the Sun Shines Nellie,* and *Under the Anheuser Bush,* wrote:

First Verse
When Louis came home to the flat
He hung up his coat and his hat,
He gazed all around, but no wifey he found
So he said, "Where can Flossie be at?"
A note on the table he spied,
He read it just once, then he cried.
It ran, "Louis, dear, it's too slow for me here,
So I think I will go for a ride."

Chorus
Meet me in St. Louis, Louis,
meet me at the fair,
Don't tell me the lights are shining
any place but there.
We will dance the Hoochee Koochee,
I will be your tootsie wootsie
If you will meet me in St. Louis, Louis,
meet me at the fair.

Second Verse

The dresses that hung in the hall
Were gone, she had taken them all.
She took all his rings and the rest of his things;
The picture he missed from the wall.
"What! moving?" the janitor said,
"Your rent is paid three months ahead."
"What good is the flat?" siad poor Louis, "read that."
And the janitor smiled as he read:

Repeat Chorus

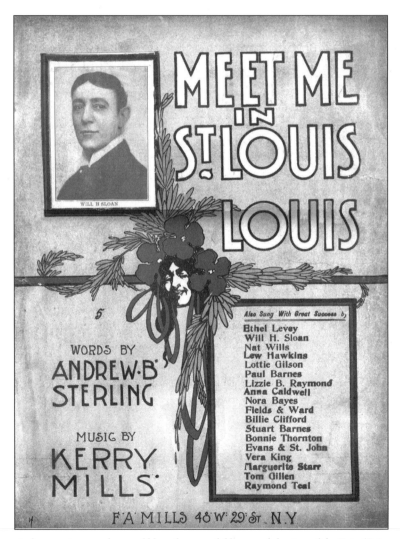

A sheet music cover that would have been available around the time of the Fair. (F.A. Mills, Publisher. From the collection of Max Storm.)

Remember Poor Louis

Mills promptly purchased Sterling's lyrics for $200 and set them to music. The popularity of *Meet Me in St. Louis, Louis* would surpass any other song inspired by the Fair, including *On The Pike*, *Strolling Down The Pike*, and Scott Joplin's *Cascades*. Ethel Levey, Lottie Gilson, Will Sloan, Nora Bayes, and other prominent vocalists of that era quickly added *Meet Me in St. Louis, Louis* to their repertoires. Billy Muarry, on the Columbia Victor label, was the first of many troubadours to put it on wax. Judy Garland's 1944 recording on the Decca label is considered a classic.

The unofficial anthem of the Louisiana Purchase Exposition is the most famous song ever written about any World's Fair. The Sterling lyric tells a compelling story. The verses set the stage for the bold invitation that Flossie extends to Louis in the chorus.

Flossie was no floozie, but a truly progressive wife taking extraordinary measures to lead her stodgy mate into the twentieth century. Consider poor Louis' predicament when he returns to his love nest and discovers that his bird in a glided cage has flown off to his namesake city. Imagine his shock upon reading that his beloved Flossie had abandoned their drab flat for the electrically-illuminated Louisiana Purchase Exposition. Flossie's 'Dear Louis' letter suddenly confronted her tootsie wootsie with the choice of remaining in the pedestrian Gilded Age or joining her in the fastlane of the Ragtime and the Hoochee Koochee era.

One can only hope that Louis accepted his spouse's invitation, and that contemporary St. Louisans will remember to sing their Fair's anthem as it was written. After all, poor Louis should never be forgotten in St. Louis.

Here are the words to the rest of the song:

3rd Verse

Lew Woods was the name of a horse, that ran at the New Orleans course,

I played him one day for a dollar each way, and I charged it to profit and loss;

He started to run in the wet, the son of a gun's running yet,

That crazy old skate, he made straight for the gate, and I hollered, "Hey Lew! don't forget."

3rd Chorus

Meet me in St. Louis, Louis, meet me at the fair,

Take my tip and don't stop running until you are there;

You're a wonder that's no liesky, if you don't fall down and diesky,

Meet me in St. Louis, Louis, meet me at the fair.

4th Verse

There came to the gay tenderloin, a Jay who had money to burn,

The poor simple soul, showed a girlie his roll, and she said, "for some wine dear, I yearn."

A bottle and bird right away, she touched him then said, "I can't stay"

He sighed, "tell me sweet where can you and I meet?" and the orchestra started to play.

4th Chorus

Meet me in St. Louis, Louis, meet me at the fair,

Don't tell me the lights are shining any place but there;

I'll be waiting there my honey, to divorce you from your money,

Meet me in St. Louis, Louis, meet me at the fair.

5th Verse

The clerks in the bank said, "it's queer, did anyone see the cashier?

It's way after time, and we haven't a dime, we can't open the safe 'till he's here."

The President shook his gray head, "send out for an expert" he said,

The door's opened wide, not a cent was inside, just a card that was all, and it read:

5th Chorus

Meet me in St. Louis, Louis, meet me at the fair,

All the boys and all the girls are going to be there;

If they ask about the cashier, you can say he cuts a dash here,

Meet me in St. Louis, Louis, meet me at the fair.

6th Verse

In church sat a man near the door, asleep, he was starting to snore,

The Minister rose, and he said, "We will close singing, Meet on the Beautiful Shore."

The man in the back then awoke, he caught the last words that he spoke;

He said, "Parson White, you can meet me alright, but The Beautiful Shore is a joke."

6th Chorus

Meet me in St. Louis, Louis, meet me at the fair,

Don't tell me the lights are shining anyplace but there;

I'll be waiting at the station, for the whole darned congregation,

Meet me in St. Louis, Louis, Meet me at the fair. ⚜

A Taste of 1904

Food at the 1904 World's Fair was more than ice cream cones, iced tea, peanut butter and puffed rice. The *World's Fair Souvenir Cookbook* by Sarah Tyson Rorer bears witness to that.

"The object of this book is twofold," she wrote in the preface. "First, to present in a compact form a few of the choice recipes used in the Eastern Pavilion ... and, secondly, to show how simply and easily all foods may be prepared."

• • • • • • • • • • • • • •
As many as 35 restaurants offered multi-course meals and the foods of many countries. Together, they could seat 36,650 people.
• • • • • • • • • • • • • •

Rorer ran a 1,200-seat restaurant at the Fair, The Model Restaurant. She also gave daily cooking demonstrations, where she sold autographed copies of her book for 50¢. Few copies survive.

From 1883 to 1903, Rorer had operated the Philadelphia School of Cooking. In all, she wrote 54 cookbooks and booklets. She edited the culinary magazine *Table Talk* from 1886 to 1893, wrote for Ladies Home Journal from 1897 to 1911 and wrote for *Good Housekeeping* in 1914 and 1915.

What seemed to be simple and easy to Rorer seems considerably more difficult today. One of her least elaborate menus was An Emergency Dinner of Canned Goods. It called for cream of tomato soup, broiled salt mackerel with parsley sauce, Lyonnaise potatoes, Timbale of macaroni with cream sauce, French omelet with peas, lettuce salad, French dressing, wafers, cheese, canned fruit and coffee.

Many people enjoyed four meals a day. They ate breakfast in the morning, lunch at noon, a substantial dinner in the late afternoon and a lighter, late evening supper. Rorer's cookbook offers daily bills-of-fare for all seasons, including the following one for spring:

Breakfast:
Baked bananas, hominy, sugar and milk, shirred eggs, plain muffins, coffee.

Lunch:
Fish cutlets, cream sauce, sliced cucumbers, brown bread, coffee.

Dinner:
Herb soup, boiled leg of mutton, caper sauce, boiled rice, stewed tomatoes, salad of watercress, wafers, cheese, caramel pudding.

Supper:
Thin slices of cold mutton, mint sauce, preserved cranberries, apples, Russian tea.

The Model Restaurant was only one of the many dining choices. Visitors to the Louisiana Purchase Exposition of 1904 could grab a quick snack from the 80 concessions that dotted the fairgrounds, or they could dine in style. As many as 35 restaurants offered multi-course meals and the foods of many countries. Together, they could seat 36,650 people.

Cafe Luzon and Cafe Michel specialized in Philippine cuisine. Diners could savor sukiyaki at Fair Japan, a variety of curries in British India, guacamole at the Mexican Restaurant and authentic Egyptian molokheya soup at The Streets of Cairo. Mr. and Mrs. McReady's Restaurant at the American Inn was noted for its "real home cooking" and wholesome family atmosphere.

Perhaps the most elegant restaurant was the Lüchow-Faust World's Fair Restaurant in the Tyrolean Alps. This restaurant was operated by Tony Faust of St. Louis and August Lüchow of New York City. The menu included such delicacies as caviar for 75¢ and filet mignon for $1.25.

The wine list included 1893 vintage Louis Roeder Brut Champagne at $6.00 a quart, and Kongil Fachingen mineral water at 65¢ a quart.

The restaurant could seat 2,500 patrons. The Tyrolean Alps hosted a banquet honoring President and Mrs. Theodore Roosevelt on November 26, 1904. The 600 guests enjoyed an elaborate banquet that included oysters, salmon souffle, medallions of beef and risotto with truffles.

The cover the the Lüchow-Faust World's Fair Restaurant Co. menu was a very colorful issustration of a Tyrolean Alps village. Note that the menu states the location of the restaurant in the Tyrolean Alps. The top of the menu advertises musical entertainment by the 100 piece Exposition Orchestra, including the titles and composers for the program. Not to miss out on additional advertising opportunities, the locations of August Lüchow's New York restaurant and Tony Faust's St. Louis restaurant were also listed. (From the collection of Bill Pieber.)

Equally pricey was The International Restaurant, operated by O.B. Abergo and A. Baroni, where 2,200 guests at a time could listen to a European orchestra and dine from an eclectic continental menu featuring many styles of spaghetti. The John Gund Brewing Co. of LaCrosse, Wisconsin spent two years preparing a special beef for The International Restaurant.

The 2,000-seat Old Parliament House in the Blarney Castle exhibit of the Irish Village was not quite so upscale. Prices ranged from 30¢ for hefty helpings of frankfurters with sauerkraut or potato salad to $1.00 for fried frog legs. John Jameson's Dublin Whiskey cost 15¢ a shot.

The two restaurants in E.M. Statler's Inside Inn offered a different kind of entertainment. The hotel accommodated 5,000 guests at a time and the two restaurants seated a total of 2,500.

With such a choice of domestic and international foods, there was no excuse for being hungry at the Fair. ⚜

The Innkeeper

In 1903, the Louisiana Purchase Exposition's promoters telegraphed a tempting offer to E. M. Statler. The Buffalo, New York restaurateur leaped at their invitation to build and operate the biggest hotel in the world. At the 1904 St. Louis World's Fair, Statler made a handsome profit and nearly lost his life.

Until 1901, Statler had been known in Buffalo as the famed restaurateur of Ellicott Square. Then he invested $60,000 in building and operating the world's largest hotel for Buffalo's Pan-American Exposition. Statler built that temporary edifice out of yellow pine, stucco, and fire-proofed burlap. His hospitality palace could accommodate up to 5,000 guests.

• • • • • • • • • • •
"The Inside Inn is
a constant joy ..."
• • • • • • • • • • •

Customers and fellow innkeepers applauded his first attempt at hotel management. A reviewer for *The Hotel Gazette* raved, "The system at Statler's is fine – bellboy,

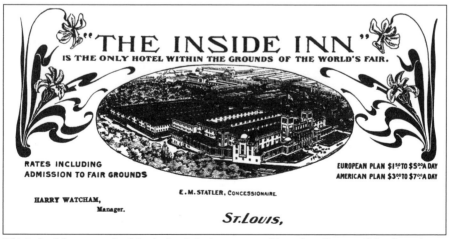

This is the elaborate masthead for the Inside Inn's stationery. (From the collection of Max Storm.)

chambermaid, dining room, and office – all perfected. Manager Statler is a wonder.

Unfortunately, the 1901 Pan-American Exposition had been a financial failure. Statler's hotel rarely sheltered more than 1,500 guests at a time. He was one of the few Pan-American Exposition entrepreneurs who didn't lose money. His efficient and frugal management methods enabled him to break even

Statler returned to his prosperous restaurant, eager to have another go at innkeeping. The St. Louis World's Fair promoters were anxious to give him that opportunity. A lack of suitable hotel accommodations had cost St. Louis the chance to host the 1893 Columbian Exposition.

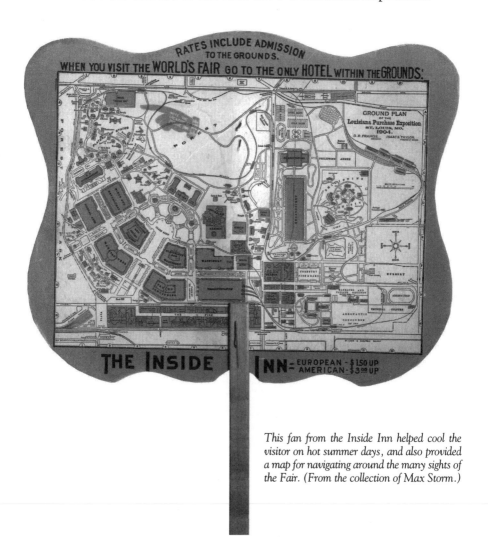

This fan from the Inside Inn helped cool the visitor on hot summer days, and also provided a map for navigating around the many sights of the Fair. (From the collection of Max Storm.)

Those St. Louisans were determined to create the grandest international exposition in history. The 1904 Olympic Games and the National Democratic Party Convention were also coming to town. They needed an innkeeper who could operate on a grand scale. Statler did not disappoint them.

This hotel far surpassed the one he had constructed for the Pan American Exposition. Statler spent six months building it out of the same materials he had used in Buffalo. John Wiley of The Hotel Monthly commented on its convenient location within the fairgrounds. At his suggestion, Statler dubbed it The Inside Inn.

The magnificent temporary structure cost $450,000, and contained two dining rooms that could seat a total of 2,500 patrons. It's 2,257 rooms could shelter up to 5,000 guests at a time, and 500 rooms had private baths. A drug store, haberdashery, shoe shine parlor, newsstand, and barber shop, were on the premises.

> This hotel far surpassed the one he had constructed for the Pan American Exposition.

Nightly rates ranged from $1.50 to $7.00, which included the Fair's daily 50¢ admission fee. Guests could choose the American or the European Plan. American Plan rates included the cost of three daily meals. On April 30, 1904, Statler's 2,000 employees were ready to serve the multitudes that flocked to the exposition's grand opening.

Statler donned formal attire, and entered his huge kitchen in route to that spectacular ceremony. Then, his chef, Louis Rosenbloom, alerted him to a problem with the kitchen's twenty gallon coffee urn. Statler, Rosenbloom, and a coffee boy bent down to investigate white puffs of smoke coming from the bottom of the boiler. Then the entire urn exploded. All three were thoroughly scalded. An ambulance rushed them to St. Anthony's Hospital.

That coffee boy, Charles Goodrich, was fatally burned. Rosenbloom, whose burns were far less serious, was hospitalized for six weeks.

While thousands of guests enjoyed his hotel's hospitality, Statler battled for his life at St. Anthony's. Doctors slowly grafted fresh skin upon his scalded legs. In late August, they let him return to the Fair in a wheel chair.

That lavish exposition lived up to Statler's greatest expectations. His hotel was constantly jammed with guests. Bellboys stationed at every corridor intersection hustled to supply them with ice water.

At the Inside Inn, Statler developed guiding principles for operating a successful hospitality establishment. He drummed up business with an unprecedented $60,000 national advertising campaign. His was the first hotel to post occupancy rates on every guest room door.

Statler was the first innkeeper to publicly promise, "... No guest will leave this house displeased. ... No employee is to be maintained who cannot please guests." He even maintained a special office to handle complaints and suggestions.

Many of his Inside Inn innovations would become standard hospitality industry practices. Customers could obtain a cheaper rate by purchasing a week's lodging in advance. Those who departed early received a partial refund. This eliminated the problem of guests skipping out on unpaid bills.

American plan guests got their meal tickets punched whenever they entered the dining room. They received refunds on any unused tickets. Many hotels, cruise ships, and resorts borrowed that idea.

This is the main entrance to the 2257 room Inside Inn. (From the collection of Max Storm.)

The Innkeeper

Statler carefully selected a capable and loyal managerial crew. His head bellman, an army veteran named Richardson, ran his bellhop operation with military precision. Mrs. Kocher and Mrs. Prince, two veteran employees from his Buffalo restaurant, solved a major crisis in the European Plan's ala carte dining room. Under that ala carte system waiters purchased meals from the kitchen and resold them to diners. Dishonest waiters divided single portions in half, and pocketed double payments from unsuspecting guests.

Kocher and Prince promptly replaced those desperados with wholesome young women. Dining room graft ceased immediately. The courteous efficiency of its white-clad waitresses became an Inside Inn trademark.

Statler's bustling hostelry became a World's Fair attraction in its own right. Collier's Weekly claimed, "The Inside Inn is a constant joy. … It is not entered on the list of exhibits, but of all the shows at the Fair, it is the most entertaining and extraordinary."

Young Theodore Roosevelt Jr. acted as the Inn's unofficial manager for a day. Little Kermit Roosevelt came down with a tummy ache after three helpings of watermelon. Boisterous national conventions of

> Statler's bustling hostelry became a World's Fair attraction in its own right.

carpenters, confectioners, undertakers, and newspaper editors, all took place under Statler's roof.

None of those spectacles surpassed the one provided by the entire West Point Cadet Corps. They all marched in to the American Plan dining room a half-hour before each regularly scheduled meal. Then, they were seated at a command. All 1,200 finished their meal in precisely 20 minutes.

Unfortunately, the Fair's attractions created nocturnal distractions for drowsy guests. Their bedrooms got the full glare of electric lights from food and entertainment concessions. Brass bands blaring World's Fair anthems kept them awake.

The cooing of honeymoon couples, the wailing of infants, and constant conversations, resounded through those thin pineboard walls. None of that kept guests and journalists from spreading the good word about the Inside Inn.

Statler made over $300,000 on his investment. After the Fair closed, he sold his temporary structure as scrap lumber for $30,000, and moved on. The Louisiana Purhase Exposition had provided him with an ideal showcase. Thousands of guests from around the world would remember Statler's establishment. The reputation he earned there helped him build his international hotel chain.

Many of the organizational principles and managerial methods pioneered at the Inside Inn are still used in the hospitality industry, and are tributes to E.M. Statler, the innkeeper of the St. Louis World's Fair. ❧

Meet Me in St. Lewis

I n 1904, people all over America sang:

> *"Meet me in St. Louis, Louis*
> *Meet me at the Fair,*
> *Don't tell me the lights are shining*
> *Any place but there ..."*

The brightest light of all was Edward Gardner Lewis' 12,000 candle-power spotlight. This brilliant beacon along with Camp Lewis, and The World's Fair Contest Company, were the three gimmicks that promoted Lewis' enterprises during the Louisiana Purchase Exposition.

• • • • • • • • • • • • • •

By all accounts, Lewis was long on sales hype and short on business ethics.

• • • • • • • • • • • • • •

Lewis' relationship with the Exposition was not one-sided. He became its self-appointed promoter. Fortune shone on St. Louis and E. G. Lewis in 1904.

This son of an Episcopal clergyman had arrived in St. Louis to peddle his dubious Anti-Skeet tablets during the summer of 1896. These tablets of salt peter and insect powder supposedly created a mosquito-repelling cloud when burned.

By all accounts, Lewis was long on sales hype and short on business ethics. Wonderful Bug Chalk, and Anti-Fly were his other insect exterminating products. Sarsaparilla Blood Medicine, Cathartic Laxative Prunes, Walk-Easy Foot Powder, Hunyadi Salts, and Dr. Hotts Cold Crackers, were among the many patented medicines on his product list. He seems to have sold everything but snake oil.

Lewis also saw lucrative prospects in magazine publishing, and purchased the *The Winner* in 1899. This magazine's offices and printing plant were in downtown

St. Louis. He soon turned it into a profitable vehicle for promoting his own products and selling advertising space.

Lewis changed the magazine's name to the Woman's Magazine in 1902. He would use the penny-per-pound postage rates and Rural Free Delivery to reach a largely rural readership. The plethora of mail order ads in the Woman's Magazine enabled him to profitably sell a year's subscription for only a dime.

Many critics considered the *Woman's Magazine* a cheap imitation of Edward Bok's *The Ladies' Home Journal*. The *Woman's Magazine* consisted mainly of recipes, household hints, and melodramatic romance stories. Lewis' regular column, *Heart to Heart with the Editor* borrowed the format that Bok had pioneered in his *Side Talk With the Girls*.

• • • • • • • • • • • •

This international exposition clearly captured Lewis' imagination.

• • • • • • • • • • • •

Lewis and his derivative journal won many hearts and subscribers. In 1904, he claimed a readership of 1,600,000 for the *Woman's Magazine*, and 600,000 for his second publishing venture, the *Woman's Farm Journal*. Lewis' figures are probably inflated, but he evidently reached an enormous public in the United States and Canada. He even offered a $100 prize to an American Post Office serving more than 50 English-speaking families where the *Woman's Magazine* did not have at least one subscriber.

A Post Office in Wyoming eventually claimed that prize. The Governor of Wyoming and his staff collected it at Lewis' headquarters during the Louisiana Purchase Exposition.

This international exposition clearly captured Lewis' imagination. In *The Siege of University City*, Sydney Morse wrote:

> "The World's Fair became the central image about which clustered all his thoughts and dreams. The Womans Magazine was perhaps the first periodical of national circulation to take up the Fair as an editorial topic. Lewis placed himself in touch with the authorities almost immediately after it was announced, and at once opened its columns as a medium of national publicity. ... Immediately, letters began to pour in from Lewis' subscribers announcing the intention of making their trip to the World's Fair the occasion of a personal visit to the editor. All sorts of questions were asked by readers. Many wanted to know about accommodations at St. Louis. Others asked about the cost and other details of transportation. Still others inquired about seasonal

and other conditions. The office of the Woman's Magazine soon became a veritable bureau of information."

Lewis could also see that his publishing enterprises were outgrowing his limited downtown facilities. He decided to relocate in the vicinity of the Exposition and the new campus of Washington University. Therefore, he purchased 85 acres of pasture land slightly west of the St. Louis city limits.

In 1903, Lewis paid his first call on David R. Francis, the President of the Louisiana Purchase Exposition. Francis would later say:

"One day, the year before the World's Fair, he sent in his card to me. … I had been so closely engaged that I really did not know of his enterprise. He told me that he was going to erect a five-story building and wanted me to lay the cornerstone. I said, 'What is it for?'

He replied, 'The publishing plant of the Woman's Magazine.'

I said, 'Have you got your money?'

He answered, 'Yes.'

'Where are you going to erect it?'

He said, 'Come to the window and I'll show you.' He pointed … from my office window.

'But,' said I, 'there is no building there.'

He replied, 'I am going to lay the cornerstone within three weeks. I will have the building up before the World's Fair.' He then showed me a circular containing the names of his directors, among them a number of men whom I knew.

I said, 'Mr. Lewis, whatever I do in my official capacity as President of the World's Fair, I must account for to the directors, to the stockholders, and to the community. I do not even know that you are going to put up your building.'

'Well,' he replied, 'how can I convince you?'

'I don't know,' said I, 'except by putting up one story and leaving the place for the cornerstone vacant. When you have done that, I will lay the cornerstone.' I thought he might take offense at that, but he only said, 'I'll do it.'

About two or three months later, Mr. Lewis paid me another visit and said, 'Well I've got that first story up. Everything is in shape, and I want you to come over and lay the cornerstone tomorrow.' I laid the cornerstone. He had complied with the conditions as I had never known another man to do under the circumstances."

On August 28, 1903 such distinquished guests as Sir Alexandrovsky, the Chamberlain to the Tsar of Russia, saw Francis lay the cornerstone for Lewis' five story octagonal office tower. Francis used that occasion to speak of Lewis' enterprise in connection with the Exposition:

> "St. Louis is attracting the attention of the world. From now on we shall take pleasure in pointing to this enterprise as one of the indications of the energy and public spirit of a St. Louisan, assisted and encouraged not only by his co-workers, but by the patronage of a million and a half subscribers throughout the United States and Canada, who read one of his publications. This is another evidence of the progressive spirit that has taken hold of the people of St. Louis. We hardly realize how prominent we are at this time in the eyes of every country on this globe. The question with us is: Shall we prove equal to our responsibilities? St. Louis is on trial, and if the people of this city are inspired by the same spirit that moves Mr. Lewis and his colleagues, St. Louis will continue to be prominent in the eyes of the world during at least the life of the present generation."

Work progressed rapidly on Lewis' office building of limestone and brick. It would stand 135 feet tall, on land 300 feet above the level of the downtown St. Louis streets. A press room building stood on the office tower's north side. Lewis' presses were rattling off copies of his periodicals by January 1, 1904. The office building was completed just in time for the Exposition's official opening on April 30.

Lewis seized that opportunity to shine his light. According to a double spread feature article that appeared in the *St. Louis Republic* newspaper during the Exposition:

> "On the night of April 30, 1904, after the dedication ceremonies opening the World's Fair, a great light suddenly burst into the sky, sweeping from the north to south and east to west in a blazing, blinding beam of seven feet in diameter, the reflection of which was seen as far away as Kansas City, nearly three hundred miles. Everyone in St. Louis wondered what it could be, and where it came from. It seemed to start from a high point in the West End of the City; and only a few of the initiated knew that it was the great search light on top of the dome of the Woman's Magazine building on University Heights. Since then it has swept the sky nightly. This light is the crowning glory of the most beautiful building in St. Louis. ... The light itself is by far the most powerful searchlight in the world, requiring nearly a year to construct. It marked the final completion of a building which probably has few equals in the world. ... This great building is open to visitors day and night."

The origins of Lewis' beacon are obscure. According to popular theory, it was constructed for the Russian pavilion at the Exposition. When Russia decided not to participate in the Exposition, Lewis was able to purchase his crowning glory at a bargain basement price.

Visitors to Lewis' 85 acres also saw the tent city he christened Camp Lewis. Lewis claimed that his encampment could accommodate from three to four thousand guests at a time, and that a total of 80,000 stayed there during the Fair.

Lewis engaged Colonel F. H. Buzzacott, a former army officer, to build and supervise his encampment. The tents for families contained amenities like board floors, iron beds with springs and mattresses, comfortable chairs, and electric lights. There were tents containing public showers and baths, reading areas, recreational equipment, and smoking areas.

A doctor and nurses staffed the Infirmary Tent. Parents could leave small children under a nurse's supervision in the Baby Tent.

Boardwalks kept the camp from turning into a mud bog on rainy days. Guests could ride to the Exposition in horse-drawn omnibuses.

A wholesome family atmosphere prevailed. Intoxicants were forbidden. Paying quests were treated to nightly campfires and musical entertainment.

General Nelson A. Miles, Commander of the United States Army, reviewed Camp Lewis during his visit to the Exposition. He reported, "It is not only most comfortable, but picturesque, and from my personal inspection appears healthful. Every department seems perfect in design and management ..."

John Thompson, a caterer from Chicago, provided 25¢ lunches and 50¢ dinners in the commissary. Lewis claims to have subsidized each meal by a nickel to see that his guests were well-fed at reasonable prices.

Guests paid the bargain rate of 50¢ per night for accommodations. Camp Lewis was advertised through a promotional booklet and ads in Lewis' magazines.

Lewis appears to have been an impeccable host. His columns inspired thousands of rustic readers to attend the Fair, but many dreaded the prospect of fending for themselves in America's fourth-largest metropolis. Their letters received personal replies from members of Lewis' staff. Subscribers who reserved spaces at Camp Lewis were mailed identification badges. Lewis' employees met incoming trains at Union

Station, and safely ushered those timid tourists to their destination.

This urban hospitality seems to have endeared Lewis to his guests. They would become some of the most enthusiastic backers of his future publications and financial projects.

Camp Lewis was open on Sundays when the Exposition was closed. Sunday tours of Lewis' lavishly-appointed office building attracted thousands of camp guests and tourists. All visitors were asked to sign a guest list and purchase subscriptions. Lewis' readership and celebrity swelled.

His third promotional gimmick, the World's Fair Contest Company, earned him an estimated profit of $85,000. It also involved him in a round of legal battles. The goal of this contest was to guess the total attendance at the Louisiana Purchase Exposition. Contestants paid the fee of 25¢ for each estimate they entered. The deadline for entries was two weeks before the Exposition's closing date of December 1, 1904.

The closest guess received the first prize of $25,000. Lesser prizes, totaling $60,000, were offered. One of them was a special $5,500 prize for the closest guess made between the dates of January 1 and May 1, 1904.

Lewis had tried to convince the Fair's directors to sponsor this contest. He advocated it as a legitimate competition that would generate national newspaper coverage for the Fair.

Contestants could base their total attendance estimates on daily attendance figures published in newspapers across the nation. Lewis claimed that the 1901 Pan-American Exposition had successfully sponsored a similar contest.

When the directors of the Louisiana Purchase Exposition declined Lewis' proposal, he took on the project himself. One of his ads for the contest claimed that it was, "a good investment. Better than stocks and bonds. ... It hardly seems reasonable that with a hundred certificates one could miss ALL of the 1, 889 cash prizes."

Many disagreed. William Jennings Bryan wrote to the Postmaster General on July 17, 1903, "... it is even more demoralizing than the ordinary lottery, because the low price of the tickets and the large capital prizes promised are more alluring to those who are susceptible to the temptations of a lottery."

Lewis later admitted to having misgivings about this enterprise. He was evidently moved by letters from readers that expressed unrealistic hopes of winning the jackpot. Lewis claimed, "I would have stopped the World's Fair Contest within two weeks after it had started if I could have done so. But I had the money up, had issued the coupons and couldn't stop it."

Assistant Circuit Attorney W. S. Hancock of St. Louis failed in his three attempts to put the World's Fair Contest Company out of business. The Post Office Department was also unsuccessful in its attempts to derail this Lewis enterprise. The contest was allowed to continue, and Lewis claimed that all prize winners were paid in full.

E. G. Lewis' legal battles were far from over. His next controversial project was the People's United States Savings Bank.

In *The Siege of University City*, Sydney Morse wrote, "The whole conception seems to have taken on its final and definite form during the summer of the World's Fair. ... Each day during the World's Fair, therefore, witnessed a constant succession of interviews between Lewis and a multitude of interested callers."

The authorities succeeded in terminating this bank by mail operation. The People's United States Bank was placed in receivership in July of 1905, after the Postmaster General issued a finding that its purposes were fraudulent.

Lewis continued to get involved in controversial enterprises. He was truly an enigma. Some dismissed him as a fraud. Many visitors to Camp Lewis would always consider him a friend.

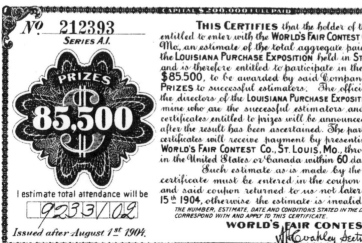

This is the front side of an entry coupon for the World's Fair Contest. (From the collection of Max Storm.)

The ground upon which Camp Lewis stood became the first subdivision of University City. Edward Gardner Lewis became its first mayor in 1906. A multitude of legal problems forced him into bankruptcy in 1911.

He resigned as mayor in 1912. Then he moved to California's San Luis Obispo County, and founded the community of Atascadero. He made and lost another fortune in California. This time his legal battles landed him behind bars. On May 1, 1928, he reported to McNeil Island Federal Prison to begin serving a six-year sentence for mail fraud. Lewis died, at the age of eighty-two, on August 10, 1950.

The legacies of E. G. Lewis and his extraordinary association with the Louisiana Purchase Exposition live in University City. His stately office building is the University City Hall. The cornerstone that David Rowland Francis planted is firmly in place.

Lewis' press building houses that community's police and fire departments. Both structures are located on Trinity Avenue, named after Lewis' Alma mater, Trinity College of Hartford, Connecticut.

Camp Lewis and the World's Fair Contest Company are long gone, but Lewis' powerful searchlight can still sweep the night sky. It occupies an honored place in the copper dome of the city hall that is a legacy of the dreams and

A FORTUNE FOR AN ESTIMATE

$85,500.00 given away in 1,891 cash prizes to those making the nearest correct estimates on the total aggregate paid attendance at the Louisiana Purchase Exposition to be held in St. Louis in 1904.

PRIZES FOR NEAREST ESTIMATE OF TOTAL PAID ATTENDANCE.

To the 1st	- - - -	$25,000 00 In Cash
To the 2nd	- - - - - -	10,000 00 "
To the 3rd	- - - - - -	5,000 00 "
To the 4th	- - - - - -	2,500 00 "
To the 5th	- - - - - -	1,500 00 "
To the 6th	-	1,000 00 "
To the next	10 nearest at $200 00 each,	2,000 00 "
To the next	20 " 100 00 each,	2,000 00 "
To the next	50 " 50 00 each,	2,500 00 "
To the next	100 " 25 00 each,	2,500 00 "
To the next	200 " 10 00 each,	2,000 00 "
To the next	500 " 5 00 each,	2,500 00 "
To the next	1,000 " 1 00 each,	1,000 00 "

Total, 1,886 prizes, amounting to $59,500 00

IN ADDITION TO THE ABOVE, THE FOLLOWING SPECIAL PRIZES WILL BE PAID:

To person making nearest correct estimate before February 1, 1903 - -	$5,500 00 In Cash
To person making nearest correct estimate between February 1, 1903, and July 1, 1903 - - - - -	5,000 00 In Cash
To person making nearest correct estimate between July 1, 1903, and January 1, 1904 - - - - - -	5,000 00 In Cash
To person making nearest correct estimate on coupons bought between January 1, 1904, and May 1, 1904 - - -	5,500 00 In Cash
To person making nearest correct estimate on coupons bought between May 1, 1904, and August 1, 1904 - - -	5,000 00 In Cash

TOTAL, 1,891 PRIZES, AMOUNTING TO $85,500.00

In case of a tie, or that two or more estimates are equally correct, prizes will be divided equally between them.

VALUABLE INFORMATION.

The total paid attendance at the World's Fair, Chicago, 1893, was 21,480,141.

The total paid attendance at the Pan-American Exposition, 1901, was 5,306,859.

The total paid attendance at the Omaha Exposition, 1898, was 1,778,250.

The contest will close Oct. 15, 1904. The names and addresses of the successful estimators will be published in the papers using this offer.

Keep this certificate in your possession until notified that the contest has been decided. Lost certificates will positively NOT be replaced.

The coupon at the end of this certificate is to be filled in with your estimate and sent to us, so as to reach us not later than midnight of October 13th, 1904.

The back of the entry coupon shows the prize information. (From the collection of Max Storm.)

schemes of Edward Gardner Lewis. The founder of University City was no St. Lewis, but his light shined bright on every night of the St. Louis World's Fair. ⚜

Buster Brown at the Fair

Buster Brown and his dog Tige, filled a big pair of shoes at the St. Louis World's Fair. Richard Fenton Outcault's popular comic strip character became the trademark for children's' footwear manufactured by the Brown Shoe Company. Generations of youngsters would hear the jingle:

> *"I'm Buster Brown.*
> *I live in a shoe!*
> *Woof! Woof! That's my dog Tige*
> *He lives in there, too ..."*

A young sales executive named John A. Bush was the man who began that marketing campaign. He was the Brown Shoe Company's representative at the Louisiana Purchase Exposition. They shared an exhibition pavilion with two other shoe manufacturing firms.

• • • • • • • • • • • • •
This international exposition became a global marketplace.
• • • • • • • • • • • • •

Those manufacturers built a model shoe factory and alternated running it in weekly intervals. St. Louis had recently become America's shoe making center. Consumers wanted to see how shoes were made in the World's Fair city.

Until 1878, no mass produced shoes came from St. Louis. That industry was based in New England. Only black shoes were made there. Mens and womens shoes looked alike.

Then 25 year old Warren G. Brown joined Alvin L. Bryan and Jerome Desnoyers to form Bryan, Brown and Company. Eventually, Bryan withdrew from that partnership and Desnoyers retired. The company acquired its present name in 1893.

By the turn of the century, it was growing at the rate of a million dollars a year. Their Home shoes for men, Gold Coin and Silver Shoes for ladies, and Blue Ribbon school shoes for boys and girls, were sold from coast to coast.

In 1897, Bush was running a hayride on his uncle's farm. Then he heard about a job opening at the Brown Company. His uncle had given him a basket of butter and chickens to take home to his mother and sisters.

Bush had another destination in mind. Basket in hand, he boarded the next train for St. Louis. Brown's Vice-President, Joseph H. Roblee, immediately offered him a job at $3.00 a week. Bush set his basket in the lobby, and went right to work as office boy and substitute elevator operator.

A souvenir advertising card from a Brown Shoe Company exhibit. (From the collection of Max Storm.)

He rapidly rose to an executive sales position. In 1899, the company's board of directors voted to back the Louisiana Purchase Exposition with a $10,000 contribution. George Warren Brown and other company executives served on many of the Fair's committees.

This international exposition became a global marketplace. Purveyors of everything from plumbing fixtures to Coca-Cola and Dr. Pepper advertised in the World's Fair Bulletin and rented booths and pavilions. Beer baron Adolphus Busch was a major underwriter of the Fair, as was the William J. Lemp Brewing Company of St. Louis, which built a huge beer hall on the fairgrounds.

On May 4, 1902, Richard Fenton Outcault introduced New York Herald readers to Robert Buster Brown, and his talking dog, Tige.

Impish Buster had a prim and proper sister named Mary Jane.

The cartoonist patterned those characters after his own youngsters and their dog. His fashionably-dressed wife served as the model for Buster's mother and her wardrobe.

That comic strip would eventually run in all the old Hearst newspapers, other American dailies, and periodicals in 76 foreign countries. Books like My Resolutions Buster Brown were instant best-sellers.

Outcault is often called, "the father of the funny papers." He created the original newspaper comic strip for the New York World in 1894. That daily had just developed the first color printing process. It's Sunday editor figured that a colorful comic page would boost circulation.

Outcault's Hogan's Alley, with its hero, the Yellow Kid, scored an immediate hit. The Yellow Kid was not a positive role model. This bald-headed, night-shirted, street urchin lived in Hogan's Alley with his pet parrot and goat.

In 1896, the New York Journal enticed Outcault to bring his strip to their Sunday comic page. The New York World countered by hiring George Luks to create a Yellow Kid clone for them. These two dailies battled for circulation. Both pandered to the masses with yellow ink and sensational headlines. More conservative competitors dubbed them Yellow Kid Journals. Thus, the term yellow journalism was born.

Outcault stopped slumming with the Yellow Kid in 1898. In 1901, he hooked up with the New York Herald, and drew a new comic strip called Pore Li'l Mose. In 1902, he abandoned that project in favor of Buster Brown.

Buster was the first wholesome comic strip hero. Middle and upper class parents approved of him. He was a lovable rascal who always resolved to mend his mischievous ways.

That colorful character became a full-fledged fad. The children of upper and middle class families affected his hair style and Lord Fauntleroy clothing.

In 1903, John A. Bush saw the value of using Buster Brown's name in the shoe business. He persuaded his boss to purchase that right from Outcault. Their first Buster Brown shoes made an impressive debut at the Louisiana Purchase Exposition. The Brown Company won the only Grand Prize Ribbon awarded to a shoe exhibitor.

Outcault was convinced that other manufacturers would want to purchase a piece of Buster. The cartoonist set up his own ad agency, and rented a booth at the St. Louis World's Fair. He peddled that trademark to at least 50 different companies at the Fair. The price ranged from $5 to $1,000 depending on his whim and the purchaser's budget.

Buster's phenomenal popularity crossed generational lines. Coffee, soda pop, wheat flour, waffle irons, whistles, watches, playing cards, cameras, shaving mugs, garters, cigars, and whiskey, were among the products marketed under his name. Of those original World's Fair clients, only the Brown Shoe Company and the Buster Brown Apparel Company are still in business.

In 1914, the Charles M. Miller Candy Company introduced a peanut butter and molasses confection named after Buster's sister. "Mary Janes" are still sold today.

Outcault retired as a comic strip artist in 1918. He devoted the rest of his life to theatrical projects, and co-authoring a Buster Brown dramatic production.

After the Louisiana Purchase Exposition, John A. Bush made a prodigious effort to promote Buster Brown Shoes. The company's early marketing campaign used the Outcault jingle, which went as follows:

> "Resolved!!!!! That I have found a shoe
> That I can recommend
> For Jane and I have tried to buy
> A shoe that's strong and stylish too
> And if you want to jump and run
> As children have to do
> Go in the store and ask the man
> for Buster Brown Blue Ribbon Shoes."

From 1904-1915, several diminutive actors regularly toured the country as Buster Brown. Many pups played the part of Tige. Four-foot two-inch Edmund Hensley, in red hat, knickers, blue tie, and white Buster-collared shirt, was the most famous Buster impersonator. Each stage show ended with the pitch, "Look for my picture in the heel."

The Brown Company had Hensley and other adults portray Buster at various times during the 1920s and 30s. In 1943, Smilin' Ed McConnell and his Buster Brown Gang premiered on the West Coast NBC radio network. McConnell brought that show to television in 1951. He continued as its host until his death in 1954. Andy Devine assumed that role in 1955. The show went off the air in less than a year.

John A.Bush was promoted to Vice President of the Brown Shoe

Company in 1912. He became its President in 1915, and Chairman of the Board in 1948. After 64 years of service, he retired.

The Brown Shoe Company still markets its childrens footwear under the Buster Brown trademark. A baseball-capped boy and his dog appear on their updated logo. They carry on the tradition of that rambunctious pair who lived in the shoes that debuted at the St. Louis World's Fair. ⚜

The World's Fair According to Geronimo

When the Indian School Band at the Louisiana Purchase Exposition struck up *The Star Spangled Banner*, A 75-year old Apache chieftain sprang to his feet, doffed his black felt hat and stood in respectful silence. His sturdy physique was stiff with arthritis. All eyes were on him. He was Geronimo.

Captain S. Sayre, the army officer in charge of Apache prisoners of war at Fort Sill, Oklahoma, delivered him to the Fair on June 6, 1904. Geronimo would reside in the Apache Village until October 2nd.

• • • • • • • • • • •
Geronimo's grizzly reputation may not have been grounded in fact.
• • • • • • • • • • •

That village was one of many tribal encampments near the Indian Building. This structure housed the Indian School for pupils of all ages, and an area of booths where artisans from different tribes worked at traditional crafts.

One booth showcased Pueblo pottery makers. Another featured a demonstration of bread making. Geronimo had his own booth, where he fashioned bows and arrows, and, occasionally performed traditional Apache dances and songs.

Visitors lined up to pay 10¢ for his autograph. Prices for his photograph ranged from 50¢ to $2.00.

He participated in the Indian anthropological exhibit presented by the U. S. Department of the Interior. Dr. S.M. McCowan, superintendent of the Indian boarding school at Chilocco, Oklahoma, was the exhibit's director.

McCowan received numerous mail order requests for Geronimo souvenirs. He replied with a fee schedule and this explanation, "The old gentleman is pretty high priced, but then he is the only Geronimo."

Brigadier General Nelson A. Miles had dubbed Geronimo, "the Red Devil." Government Indian agent, Woodworth Clum, had labeled him, "… the greatest single-handed murderer in American history." An Oklahoma politician had claimed that Geronimo possessed, "between eighty-five and one hundred white scalps … also a vest made of the hair of the whites whom he has killed."

Geronimo's grizzly reputation may not have been grounded in fact. The testimony of one of his comrades on the warpath

A souvenir post card. (From the Collection of Max Storm.)

suggests that the outnumbered Apaches only took lives in self-defense, "… Anybody who saw us would kill us, and we did the same thing. We had to if we wanted to live."

In his later life, Geronimo chose to follow an entirely different path as a convert to Christianity.

The road that led to his conversion began when he and his band of 16 warriors, 14 women, and six children, surrendered to General Miles at Skeleton Canyon, Arizona on September 4, 1886. Newspapers from coast to coast ran headlines like "APACHE WAR ENDED" and "GERONIMO CAPTURED."

Geronimo's band and 394 other Apaches became prisoners of war. The latter group included Geronimo's wife and children and some of the scouts who had helped Miles track him down.

All were shipped by rail to Fort Pickens, Florida. On May 13, 1888,

The Woirld's Fair According to Geronimo

the War Department transferred them to Mount Vernon Barracks, Alabama.

The hot humid climate was responsible for an alarmingly-high death rate among these Arizonans. Dr. Walter Reed, Mount Vernon's post surgeon, strongly recommended their transfer to a drier location in the Southwest.

On October 4, 1894, they were moved to Ft. Sill, Oklahoma, an army post near Lawton. The Apache prisoners were allotted farmland bordering the Comanche, Kiowa, and Kiowa-Apache reservations.

The Reformed Church in America carried out missionary work among Ft. Sill's Apache prisoners. Rev. Frank Hall Wright, a Choctaw Indian, came to the area in 1895. He was later joined by Dr. Walter C. Roe. Miss Maud Atkinson arrived in 1899 to serve as mission school teacher, nurse and home visitor.

At first, Geronimo only favored their ministry to children. "I, Gerinomo, and these others are now too old to travel your Jesus road. But our children are young and I and my brothers will be glad to have the children taught about the white man's God."

But, during the summer of 1902, he attended a Sunday camp meeting, and sat in the front row with his slender hands folded on his lap.

Near the end of the meeting, he stood up and proclaimed that the "Jesus road" was best. Then he said, "Now we begin to think that the Christian white people love us."

Geronimo continued to attend services at the mission. In July of 1903, he went to a series of camp meetings. At the end of the final meeting, he stood up and declared, "I am full of sins, and I walk alone in the dark. I see that you missionaries have got a way to get sin out of the heart, and I want to take that better road and hold it till I die."

He was baptized one week later. The missionaries at his baptism recalled that, "… his face softened and became bright with joy."

During his years at Ft. Sill, many promoters offered him substantial public appearance fees. The War Department screened all invitations, and only allowed him to travel under military guard.

He took part in the Indian exhibits at the Trans-Mississippi Exposition in Omaha in 1898 and Buffalo's 1901 Pan-American Exposition. He could barely print fast enough to accommodate autograph seekers. Buttons from his jacket sold for 25¢. His hat cost $5.00.

He continually replenished his supply of both items.

Geronimo dictated his memoirs to Stephen Melvil Barrett, Lawton's superintendent of Education, in 1905. An entire chapter of Geronimo's *Story of His Life* is devoted to his recollections of the Louisiana Purchase Exposition.

Geronimo didn't choose to recall his impressions of Omaha and Buffalo. As Barrett explained in a footnote, "Geronimo was also taken to both the Omaha and Buffalo Expositions, but during that period of his life he was sullen and took no interest in things. The St. Louis Exposition was held after he had adopted the Christian religion and had begun to try to understand our civilization."

Indians that were part of the Indian anthropological exhibit presented by the U. S. Department of the Interior. ("St. Louis World's Fair Sights, Scenes and Wonders", The Crowell Publishing Company. From the collection of Ron Schira.)

Many people came to the Fair to study "primitive cultures." University of Chicago anthropology students did field work there. Dr. Starr of that university taught "The Louisiana Purchase Exposition Class in Ethnology" on the Fairgrounds.

Dr. William F. Slocum, the President of Colorado College, considered the Fair, "... as perfect an illustration as has been seen of the method of the university of the future, which is to exchange pictures and living objects for textbooks."

Geronimo came to the Fair as a representative of a "primitive culture." His Christian conversion inspired him to learn the strange ways of "the white man's civilization."

He strolled The Pike in the company of his guards many times. "When people first came to the Fair they did nothing but parade up and down the streets. When they got tired of this they would visit the shows," he recalled.

The warrior, who was nicknamed The Tiger of the Human Race, wouldn't hazard a ride called Shooting the Chutes. "People were getting into a clumsy canoe upon a tiny shelf, and sliding down into the water. They seemed to enjoy it, but it looked too fierce for me."

The Pike's exhibit of Glass Weavers fascinated him. "I had always thought that these things were made by hand, but they were not. The man had a curious little instrument, and whenever he would blow through this into a little blaze the glass would take any shape he wanted it to. I am not sure, but I think that if I had this kind of instrument I could make whatever I wished ... But I suppose it is very difficult to get these instruments or other people would have them ... I bought many curious things in there ..."

He marveled at a trained bear's intelligence, "... In one of the shows, a man had a white bear who was as intelligent as a man. He would do whatever he was told – carry a log on his shoulder, just as a man would; then, when he was told, put it down again ... I am sure that no grizzly bear could be trained to do these things."

The grizzled chieftain didn't know quite what to make of a puppet show. "In front of us were some strange little people who came out on the platform They did not seem in earnest about anything they did; so I only laughed at them."

As a practicioner of ancient Apache medicine, he saw magic shows as demonstrations of an unearthly power. "... There was a strange looking Negro. The manager tied his hands fast, then tied him to a chair ... He twisted in his chair for a moment, and then stood up; I do not understand how this was done. It was certainly a miraculous power, because no man could have released himself by his own efforts."

> • • • • • • • • • • • • • • •
> **As a practitioner of ancient Apache medicine, he saw magic shows as demonstrations of an unearthly power.**
> • • • • • • • • • • • • • • •

The electrical energy that powered the Ferris Wheel also intrigued him. "One time the guards took me into a little house that had four windows. The little house started to move along the ground. I was scared, for our house had gone high up in the air, and the people down in the Fair Grounds looked no larger than ants. I had never been so high in the air, and I tried to look into the sky. Then they said, 'Get out!', and when I looked we were on the street again. After we were safe on the land I watched many of these little houses going up and coming down, but I cannot understand how they travel. They are curious little houses."

After seeing Turks conduct a mock battle with scimitars, he described them as, "strange men with red caps", and concluded, "they would be hard people to kill in a hand-to-hand fight."

As a representative of a Native American culture, his observations of the Igorotes Village at the Philippine Reservation are particularly interesting. "There were some little brown people at the Fair that the United States troops captured recently on some islands far from here. They did not wear much clothing and I think that they should not have been allowed to come to the Fair. But they themselves did not seem to know any better. They had some little brass plates, and they tried to play music with these. They danced to this noise and seemed to think they were giving a fine show. I heard that the President sent them to the Fair so that they could learn some manners, and when they went home teach their people how to dress and how to behave."

During his stay in St. Louis, Geronimo made frequent appearances in the Cummins Wild West Show on The Pike and, on several Sundays, in Colonel Zach Mulhall's Wild West Shows at the Delmar Race Track. He recalled these experiences, "The President of the Fair sent for me to go to a wild west show. I took part in the roping contests before the -audience. There were many other Indian tribes there, and strange people of whom I have never heard."

• • • • • • • • • • • • • • •
...his observations of the Igorote Village at the Philippine Reservation are particularly interesting.
• • • • • • • • • • • • • • •

Geronimo concluded his World's Fair reminiscences, "I am glad I went to the Fair. I saw many interesting things and learned much of the white people. They are a kind and peaceful people. During all the time I was at the Fair no one tried to harm me in any way. I wish all my people could have attended the Fair."

Dr. McCowan had known Geronimo before his religious awakening. When Geronimo was about to leave St. Louis, McCownan reported to Captain Sayre at Ft. Sill, "he really has endeared himself to Whites and Indians alike. With one or two exceptions, when he was not feeling well, he was gentle, kind and courteous. I did not think I could ever speak so kindly of the old fellow whom I have always regarded as an incarnate fiend. I am very glad to return him to you in as sound and healthy condition as when you brought him here."

Geronimo continued to make public appearances, including a dramatic display of horsemanship in President Theodore Roosevelt's inaugural parade on March 4th, 1905. Spectators threw their hats in the air and yelled, "Hooray for Geronimo!" When asked why he had requested Geronimo's participation, Roosevelt replied, "I wanted to give the people a good show."

Five days later, Geronimo visited the White House. He asked the President to allow the Apache prisoners to return to Arizona. Roosevelt listened compassionately, but political pressures prevented him from granting that request.

Geronimo's admiration of the President was undiminished. He dedicated his memoirs to him, and said in its chapter on religion, "… I am glad to know that the President of the United States is a Christian, for without the help of the Almighty I do not think that he could rightly judge in ruling so many people …"

The Louisiana Purchase Exposition was the last World's Fair Geronimo attended. He died on February 17, 1909. Congress finally released his fellow prisoners on August 24, 1912.

In 1904, a writer in Harper's Magazine commented, "remember that such a Fair as this that St. Louis offers leaves no intelligent visitor where it found him. It fills him full of pictures and of knowledge that keep coming up in his mind for years afterward. It gives him new standards, new means of comparison, new insight into conditions of life in the world he is living in."

An extraordinarily intelligent visitor named Geronimo opened his mind to the pictures, knowledge, and insights, he would share in the chapter of his life's story devoted to the St. Louis World's Fair. ⚜

The Culinary Culture Clash

On April 17, 1904, the Philippine Commissioners of the Louisiana Purchase Exposition honored their promise to the Igorote tribe. Over 100 of those headhunters had traveled 10,000 miles from northern Luzon. The commissioners had promised that they would have "... everything their hearts and stomachs desired ...," once they reached St. Louis. The Igorotes declared their intense desire for dog meat.

••••••••••••
"The Igorotes have been complaining about not receiving any dogs for eating."
••••••••••••

The Igorotes only allowed their adult males to consume canine flesh. They believed it enhanced their headhunting prowess. In Louisiana and the Fair, Dr. J.W. Buel commented on that tribe's extreme passion for dog meat, "... To obtain this food they will barter any of their possessions except human skulls ... they seem to suffer when it is not procurable."

Those tribesmen were deprived of dogs during their first weeks in St. Louis. On March 29, the commissary department of the exposition's Philippine Commission applied to the St. Louis pound master to "supply a number of dogs daily for the canine-eating tribe of Igorotes, now quartered at the Cuartel

Preparing the feast. ("Photographs of The Fair 1904" published by the Educational Company. From the collection of Yvonne Suess.)

de Filipino on the fairgrounds." The pound master agreed to accommodate them. Then the St. Louis Humane Society threatened to enforce the city's ordinance against cruelty to animals. That put the kibosh on any fido feast until the tribe moved to the Fair's 40 acre Philippine Exhibit on April 17. Their new habitation was located a few hundred feet beyond the city's limits and the Humane Society's jurisdiction.

On April 14, the commissioners requisitioned six 18 inch iron pots for that April 17 banquet. They politely requested that the Igorotes refrain from their unsightly custom of roasting whole pups over burning coals in an open pit. The famished headhunters obliged their hosts.

This culinary controversy made national headlines. Dr. T.K. Hunt, Governor of the Philippine Exhibit, received letters from many Missourians eager to supply those tribesmen with dogs. Mortimer T. Jeffers of Dexter, Missouri made this truly selfless offer:

> "The Igorotes have been complaining about not receiving any dogs for eating. ... I put in many a weary day in their own country and many a day while there I had yearned for a few bites of those dishes which I left back in the good old state of Missouri. This has won my sympathy for the poor, disconsolate wretches separated from the rations which they were reared upon ... I will send you as many dogs as you can use, up to the number of 200. I seek no remuneration whatever except that you pay the freight."

No record of Dr. Hunt's reply exists. In fact, there is no official record of how the Igorotes were supplied with the dogs they publicly consumed during their stay in the Philippine Exhibit.

Those headhunters were among the 1,100 Philippine natives who resided there in several different tribal villages. Fairgoers paid 50¢ to see inhabitants of the islands that America had annexed after the Spanish-American War.

In his narrative reminiscence, *A Boy At the Fair*, Edward J. Goff wrote that the Igorotes "... would have stray dogs brought to them and kept in a pen for their use for food. ... I did finally succeed one day in seeing them butcher a small dog; cut it up in pieces and cook it in a large iron pot together with vegetables ... they passed around plates to the -visitors, but nobody took any."

The Igorotes mastered iron pot canine cookery. They convivially invited such distinguished visitors as Secretary of War William Howard

Taft to share their favorite delicacy. There is no report that the Igorotes took offense, or skulls, when visitors declined to dine with them.

Some undocumented accounts suggest that the tribe was supplied 20 pups per day by the St. Louis Dog Pound. I doubt that the diligent St. Louis Humane Society would have allowed any city pooches to end up in those iron pots. Nor is there any authoritative evidence to support the local legend that those tribesmen risked arrest to forage for dogs in St. Louis neighborhoods.

This man, in need of money, is taking his dogs to the Philippine Exhibit to sell to the Igorotes. ("Photographs of The Fair 1904" published by the Educational Company. From the collection of Yvonne Suess.)

The written accounts of several eye witnesses clearly state that people willingly brought dogs to the Igorote Village. The exhibit was located within the suburb of Clayton. The St. Louis Humane Society had no legal authority there. Many Clayton residents saw no reason to deprive the Igorotes of the food that was so important to them. Those canines had to come from someplace. Clayton seems like the best bet.

A group of young Clayton men established a club called The Ancient Order of Igorotes. The football team of Clayton's Wydown School bears that tribal name. However, there is no conclusive evidence that any of Clayton's permanent residents took up dog-eating or headhunting.

The Louisiana Purchase Exposition closed on December 1, 1904.

The written accounts of several eye wittnesses clearly state that people willingly brought dogs to the Igorote Village.

The Igorotes quickly departed for home. That tribe had been imported to St. Louis as part of an anthropological exhibit. The World's Fair promoters wanted to give visitors their first opportunity to see how Igorotes really lived.

The Igorotes were one of over 50 ethnic and tribal villages exhibited at that truly international exposition. Visitors marveled at seeing the representatives of so many different national and cultural groups. Food is essential to all cultures. People are naturally curious about what other people eat.

Many journalists who visited the Fair wrote about the Moros' fondness for crayfish and embryo chickens, the African Pygmies' craving for monkey and elephant flesh, and the Pantagonians' preference for horse, ostrich, and guanaco. Numerous visitors gaped at the sight of South African Kaffirs broiling worms and grasshoppers over glowing coals. Recipes for such native delectables do not appear in Mrs. Rorer's cookbook, but none of them created an apparent controversy. The St. Louis Humane Society never formally expressed concern about the welfare of those worms and grasshoppers.

The Igorotes could have eaten everything from ox tails to escargot without anyone raising an objection. They never intended to offend

This illustration of the Philippine Village shows the grand scale of the complex. (From the collection of Max Storm.)

The Culinary Culture Clash

their hosts. How were they to know that their favorite food was America's sacred cow?

The breasts of adult male Igorotes were tattooed with a record of all the skulls they had captured in combat. I suppose they resumed their headhunting ways when they returned to Luzon. They probably ate the same food to prepare for battle. I wonder if they considered those skirmishes trivial compared to the culinary culture clash at the St. Louis World's Fair. ⚜

A Living Souvenir

Lively conversation comes naturally to ninety year old Frances. She participated in one of the liveliest exhibitions on The Pike. That's what people called the mile long amusement area at the St. Louis World's Fair. Frances never snacked on The Pike's renowned ice cream cones, iced tea, fruit juice icicles, frankfurters or peanut butter. A special infant formula nourished her. She was one of the premature infants who battled for their lives in the Baby Incubator Exhibit.

● ● ● ● ● ● ● ● ● ● ● ●

St. Louis World's Fair visitors witnessed the scientific process as well as it's outcome.

● ● ● ● ● ● ● ● ● ● ● ●

Other expositions had merely showcased finished products. St. Louis World's Fair visitors witnessed the scientific process as well as it's outcome. At the Baby Incubator Exhibit, they saw an invention actually saving human lives.

An interior view of the Baby Incubator Exhibit on the Pike. The 50¢ admission cost helped cover the cost of caring for babies that received care as part of the exhibit. ("St. Louis World's Fair Sights, Scenes and Wonders", The Crowell Publishing Company. From the collection of Ron Schira.)

Premature infants had little hope of survival before Dr. Alan M. Thomas and Dr. William Champion constructed the first infant incubator in 1888. A Tennessean named E.M. Bayliss brought this first public exhibition of their invention to the St. Louis World's Fair. All of those infants came from local orphan asylums and impoverished families. The cost of their care was entirely underwritten by the exhibit's 20¢ admission fee. Thousands gladly paid that price to hear lectures on the latest innovations in infant care while witnessing them in action.

Frances weighed 2 lbs. 11 oz. when a St. Louis policeman brought her there on a sweltering July 1, 1904. The young patrolman had marveled at that exhibit on his first visit to the Fair. When he found the abandoned baby on his beat, he knew just where to take her.

St. Louis physician, Dr. Joseph P. Hardy, directed a staff of ten trained nurses. The 14 metal-framed glass incubators were housed in The Pike's only fire-proof structure. Each stood three feet off the floor, on four iron support posts. Ventilating pipes constantly supplied the babies with heated fresh air. A small revolving wheel inside each incubator revealed the infant's rate of oxygen consumption.

Frances lived in her incubator for nearly two months. Every morning, a nurse unswathed her soft cotton bandages and gently dusted her with a fine rice powder. As she grew stronger, nurses began wrapping her in heated blankets and feeding her on their laps.

When Dr. Hardy considered her ready to endure normal temperatures, she graduated to a tiny enamel crib in the exhibit's glass-enclosed nursery. That's where she slurped her first bottled milk, and acquired the pinkness that still illuminates her face.

The policeman who had rescued Frances brought his new bride to the Fair many times. They got off at all 17 stops on the Fair's electric Intramural Railroad to witness demonstrations of such extraordinary inventions as heavier-than-air flying machines, coin changers, electric clocks, and automatic telephone answering machines.

On The Pike they met a young cowboy storyteller named Will Rogers. At the Apache Village, they saw the elderly chieftain Geronimo shaking hands with the visiting sons of President Theodore Roosevelt. In the evenings they rode the 250 foot Ferris Wheel, and beheld the electrically-illuminated fairscape.

Frances was their favorite Fair attraction. On each visit they rejoiced at her miraculous progress. When the Fair closed, they took her home as their adopted daughter. That day, December 1, 1904, was declared David Rowland Francis Day in honor of the Louisiana Purchase Exposition's president. They named Frances after him.

Frances loved listening to her parents' reminiscences about her first home. Nearly all of the Fair's buildings were gone by the time they took her back to the fairgrounds. Her parents nostalgically pointed out the places where they had gaped at everything from a 25 foot high soap bubble fountain to spectacular reenactments of the Boer War.

Those events came to life for Frances through the memories of her mother and father. Years later, hearing Will Rogers on the radio reminded her that her parents had seen him at the 1904 World's Fair. When her children, grandchildren, and great grandchildren, were born, she thought of all those fairgoers who were awe-struck by the miracle they saw in her.

On a steamy summer day, 90 years later, Frances sipped cool iced tea while strolling the former fairgrounds. Lingering at the site of the giant Ferris Wheel, she recalled what her parents told her about the Fair's magnificent culminating event. Just before midnight, on December 1, 1904, David Rowland Francis took one last look at its luminous treasures and wished, "they might live forever."

Then, Frances remembered that her parents fondly called her their World's Fair souvenir. For them, the Fair lived through her. As I listened to that vivacious namesake of

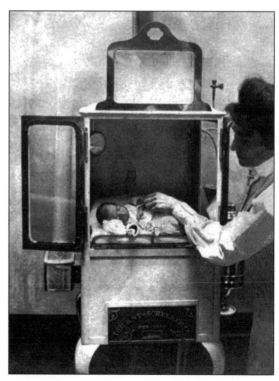

A close-up view of one of the nurses caring for a baby in the Baby Incubator Exhibit on the Pike. ("St. Louis World's Fair Sights, Scenes and Wonders", The Crowell Publishing Company. From the collection of Ron Schira.)

David Rowland Francis, I felt the spirit that moved St. Louis in 1904. Whenever I think of that lively great-grandmother, I feel the life of the St. Louis World's Fair. ⚜

Memories of Labor Day 1904

Whenever Emma Sprague of St. Louis heard the Star Spangled Banner, she remembers Labor Day 1904 – Monday, September 5. Six year old Emma and her parents were among the thousands of Labor Day celebrants at the St. Louis World's Fair.

• • • • • • • • • • •
The electric lights of every exposition building shone that evening.
• • • • • • • • • • •

The holiday agenda was packed with patriotic parades and concerts featuring military drill teams and marching bands from all 45 states. The electric lights of every exposition building shone that evening, as spectacular cascades of fireworks saluted the holiday.

One memory of that celebration outshines all the others in Emma's mind. She can still picture herself sitting in the afternoon sun, with a red-white-and-blue paper fan in one hand and her very first ice cream cone in the other, while enjoying the student marching drill and band concert on the Indian Government School grounds.

The school was part of the exhibit of Native American

"Reflected glories of the night illuminations of Festival Hall and Cascades." (From a stereo view by Underwood & Underwood. From the collection of Yvonne Suess.)

tribal villages sponsored by the U.S. Department of Interior. These students from many tribes were the first Native Americans she had even seen.

After the school's drill team retreated from the parade ground the band struck up *The Star Spangled Banner.* American audiences were not yet expected to stand during performances of the song that would not become the national anthem until 1931.

> The eyes of the audience soon turned from the musicians as the grandstands buzzed with whispers of recognition.

But an elderly Apache chief proudly rose to his feet, stiff with arthritis, doffed his black felt hat, and respectfully fixed his eyes on the stars and stripes flying from the flag pole. The eyes of the audience soon turned from the musicians as the grandstands buzzed with whispers of recognition. Then Emma's wide-eyed parents whispered to one another, "It's Geronimo!"

They knew his wrinkled face from the many pictures that had appeared in St. Louis newspapers since his arrival from the Apache reservation near Ft. Sill, Oklahoma on June 6, 1904. The Apaches had surrendered to federal troups in Arizona in 1886, and were still held as prisoners of war. Geronimo was participating in the Department of Interior's exhibit with the permission of President Theodore Roosevelt.

Celebrity-struck souvenir hunters surrounded Geronimo immediately after the concert. A parasol-shaded matron offered $5 for his hat, and a cigar-chomping Baltimore businessman proposed to pay $2 to have his picture taken with the man he called the one and only Geronimo.

The dignified chief maintained stern-faced silence until a young

"Machinery Building at night." (From a stereo view by H.C. White Co. From the collection of Yvonne Suess.)

Memories of Labor Day 1904

man, identifying himself as a Chicago newspaper reporter, inquired, "Will you ever go back on the war path?" Geronimo gazed upon "Old Glory" and simply said, "Now I see that this way is best. This is the way for my children."

Emma remembered these words and the celebrated Apache whose name her only child, Anthony, would shout whenever he parachuted into combat at a Corporal in the 82nd Airborne Division during World War II.

Even as a 97 year old great-grandmother, stiff with arthritis, Emma would proudy rise to *The Star Spangled Banner* and her memory of Labor Day 1904. ⚜

Will and Betty Rogers' World's Fair Date

In September 1904, Will Rogers got a letter from Betty Blake, a young woman he hadn't seen in over four years. The 25 year old Oklahoman was in St. Louis performing with Colonel Zach Mulhall's Congress of Rough Riders and Ropers. Betty, her sister, and a friend were visiting the St. Louis World's Fair. She happened to overhear people raving about the roping prowess of a cowboy showman named Will Rogers. Betty took the words "Meet me in St. Louis" to heart. The well mannered rural lass made a courageous move. She boldly obtained his local address, and wrote to ask if he'd like to renew their acquaintance. Betty's epistle reached him at Mulhall's 4643 Washington Boulevard home.

• • • • • • • • • • •
Betty took the words Meet me in St. Louis to heart.
• • • • • • • • • • •

Their first encounter had occurred in the late Autumn of 1899. Will operated his father's cattle ranch near Oologah, Oklahoma. Miss Blake had just arrived from the town of Rogers, Arkansas. She had recently recovered from typhoid fever. Her mother thought that visiting Oklahoma would lift her spirits.

Betty's sister was married to Oologah's Missouri Pacific railroad agent. Will frequented vaudeville theaters on his cattle selling trips to Kansas City. He kept up on all the latest urban music and dance crazes. The ethnic songs popularized by the musical team of Bert Williams and George Walker had become his passion. Will and Betty saw one another when he came to the train station to pick up the banjo he had ordered from Kansas City. They exchanged no words.

A few nights later, the Ellis family invited Will and Betty to dinner at the hotel they owned in Oologah. After dessert, Will took out a roll of sheet music and treated everyone to acappella tenor renditions of Williams and Walker standards.

A wholesome evening of corn-popping and taffy-rolling followed his serenade. Betty mentioned that she played the piano. Will wanted to hear her play the tunes he had sung. They made a date for Will to bring his sheet music and banjo to her sister's home. Will was immediately impressed with Betty's skill at both the piano and banjo. Music became their common ground.

Will Rogers signed this photo, "Yours for fun." This publicity photo is probably from late in his career. (From the collection of Ron Schira.)

They saw a lot of each other during Betty's trip to Oologah. In December, she returned to Arkansas. They exchanged a few letters during the winter and spring of 1900. When Will entered a September rodeo in Springfield, Missouri, they had a brief reunion in the grandstands.

Later that fall, they separately attended a week long street fair in Fort Smith, Arkansas. Each knew that the other was in town, but they never got together. Betty would write about that fair's final event, "I kept looking for him all during the evening, and finally, as I danced by a window, I saw him wandering around among the people outside on the cool green lawn. He was watching the dancers and sometimes glancing in my direction. But he did not come in and I did not go out."

Will set his sights on becoming a rodeo champion. On July 4, 1899, he won the $18.50 first prize in a steer-roping contest in Claremore, Oklahoma. That October, he participated in another roping competition at the old St. Louis Fair Grounds. Colonel Zach Mulhall, the general livestock agent for the San Francisco Railroad, orchestrated that event.

Mulhall was born in 1847 and orphaned as an eight year old. An aunt and uncle raised him in St. Louis. During his long railroad career, he became fascinated with cattle ranching and the western prairies.

In 1889, he joined the sooners who rushed in to Oklahoma when Cherokee lands were opened to outsiders. He was among the founders of the Oklahoma town that bears his last name. His fellow settlers gave him the honorary title, Colonel.

That Oklahoma colonel had a lot of P. T. Barnum in him and a flair for self-promotion. In 1900, Will took part in his wild west show at the reunion of Teddy Roosevelt's Rough Riders in Oklahoma City. Roosevelt, who was running for Vice-President on William McKinley's ticket, applauded Mulhall's production. By his account he became Roosevelt's confidant. He dropped Roosevelt's name at every opportunity. Mulhall's teenage daughter, Lucille, had become an expert roper and rider. He often boasted that Roosevelt urged him to take her on a national performance tour.

Will performed in many Mulhall productions. The Colonel was the first promoter to present demonstrations of real cowboy skills as public entertainment. One of his handbills proclaimed, "The contestants in this carnival are in no case professional show people, but on the other hand present the best in their class as found in each instance pursuing their vocations."

Those extravaganzas also included the Frisco Cowboy Band. That group of over 60 musicians was sponsored by the Colonel's railroad employers. Mulhall used his ties with Roosevelt to arrange for them to perform at President McKinley's inauguration.

Will soon realized that earning a living at competitive cattle roping was easier said than done. That led him to try his hand at cattle ranching on the Argentine pampas. After squandering his $3000 grubstake on that venture, he headed for South Africa.

He returned to show business there as a member of Texas Jack's Wild West Show. The Cherokee Kid became his stage moniker. Australia was the next stop on his itinerary. That's where he hooked up with the Wirth Brothers Circus. They dressed him in a gold-embroidered red velvet suit. Australians and New Zealanders proclaimed him America's champion Mexican Cowboy.

In April 1904, he returned to Oklahoma. Colonel Mulhall had arranged to put on a wild west show at the old St. Louis Fair Grounds. County fairs had often been staged there. Mulhall planned his independent production to run concurrently with the World's Fair.

Mulhall had renamed his troupe The Mulhall Congress of Rough Riders and Ropers. He invited Will to join a stellar cast that included his daughters, Lucille and Mildred, and a handsome Pennsylvanian named Tom Mix.

The Colonel ballyhooed his enterprise in all the St. Louis newspapers. He informed reporters that he expected President Roosevelt to attend. Such bravado attracted the attention of Frederick T. Cummins. That colorful gentleman operated an official Louisiana Purchase Exposition concession called The Cummins Indian Congress and Wild West Show.

His five acre concession was located just off the exposition grounds, and had an entrance on The Pike. He tried to take advantage of that arrangement during the Fair. All Pike concessions were expected to close on Sundays. Cummins tried to circumvent that rule by closing his entrance on The Pike. Sunday audiences would enter through a gate located off the official World's Fair grounds.

> • • • • • • • • • • • • • • • •
> **Rogers was one-quarter Cherokee, and appreciated the irony of being cast as the last Cavalry man to die in Custer's Last Stand.**
> • • • • • • • • • • • • • • • •

This international exposition did not neglect western Americana. Borax Bill regularly drove his 20 Mule Team through the Plateau of States. The actual cabin where Theodore Roosevelt lived as a rancher was part of North Dakota's exhibit. Frederick Remington's heroic statue, *Cowboys Shooting Up a Western Town* graced The Pike's main entrance.

Mulhall's cast became part of Cummins' concession. In keeping with the exposition's educational mission, Cummins touted his ambitious production as a historical, ethnological, industrial exhibition. It featured 850 Native Americans, including, "14 high chiefs of the North American Indians." Audiences also relished the spectacle of "250 cowboys and cowgirls."

Rogers was one-quarter Cherokee, and appreciated the irony of being cast as the last Cavalry man to die in Custer's Last Stand. He had honed his showmanship during stints with Texas Jack and the Wirth Brothers. His lariat skills dazzled Pike audiences. The show attracted large crowds. Will seemed happy in St. Louis. When his father wrote to ask if he wanted to buy land in Oklahoma, he replied, "I am out of debt and going to stay as long as I can."

Will anticipated steady employment in that production until the scheduled closing of the World's Fair on December 1, 1904. His plans suddenly had to change when Colonel Mulhall wounded three men in a real shoot-out on The Pike.

A few minutes after 10 p.m. on Saturday, June 18, a huge audience exited the Wild West Show. The Pike was jammed with foot traffic. Megaphones, horns, drums, trumpets, bells and explosions from a mock naval battle created a deafening din, and Colonel Mulhall came out of his show with two of his children, Lucille and Charles. Then he saw Frank Reed who looked after the horses in that production. The two had recently quarreled over Reed's use of a Mulhall cowhand to roundup stray horses.

Mulhall and Reed had been involved in other St. Louis shootings. Three years earlier the Colonel had resided on Longfellow Boulevard. Late one evening, police found him standing on his sidewalk with a smoking revolver in his hand. A trembling pedestrian accused the Colonel of shooting at him. No charges were ever filed.

In 1898, Reed was the intended target of a shooting by a St. Louisan named John Daly. Reed and a lady companion were coming out of an infamous St. Louis saloon. Daly's bullet missed him and killed that young woman.

Amid all the hubbub on the Pike, Mulhall and Reed angrily confronted one another. Mulhall drew a revolver from his pocket. Hundreds of bystanders began fleeing in all directions. Reed was unarmed. John Muarry, another wild west show cowboy, tried to play the role of peace maker. He joined Reed in attempting to pry that revolver from Mulhall's grip. A gunshot rang out. Muarry took a bullet in the abdomen. Then the Colonel pushed Reed away and shot him in the arm. His third shot went through the side of Reed's neck.

An 18 year old St. Louisan named Ernest Morgan was among the last customers to leave the Wild West show. He unsuspectingly wandered into Mulhall's line of fire. That third bullet lodged in Morgan's abdomen.

A horse-drawn police patrol wagon arrived along with two ambulances from the exposition's Emergency Hospital which was located on the Fair's Model Street. That hospital served as many as 100 patients a day. Most were seen for minor ailments. Patients were rarely kept there overnight. The ambulances hustled the three wounded mem to the hospital. Muarry and Reed would quickly recover from their wounds. Morgan's wounds were far more serious.

Mulhall was arrested at the scene of the shooting and rushed to the World's Fair police station. Many prominent citizens offered to post bail for him. The Police tried to hold Mulhall until they knew whether or not to charge him with murder in the Morgan shooting. On Sunday he was held at St. Louis' Four Courts Jail where he received over 200 visitors. On Monday, June 20, he was released on a $20,000 bond put up by his friend Edward Butler.

The Sunday, June 19, headline in the *St. Louis Republic* read, "ZACH MULHALL SHOOTS THREE IN CROWD ON PIKE; YOUTH WILL DIE." Dr. L.H. Laidley, the exposition's medical director, personally treated Morgan. For three days that young man's condition was considered very serious. The excellent care he received from Dr. Laidley and the Emergency Hospital staff was widely credited with saving his life.

Frank Reed told the St. Louis Globe Democrat, "I expect Mulhall will get the best of it, for he has powerful friends. ... I can get 500 witnesses to testify that Mulhall was entirely to blame and that he shot Morgan." Evidently Reed understood the power of political connections and public opinion.

St. Louisans considered Reed an unsavory character. Mulhall was widely regarded as a warm-hearted and generous public figure. His proclivity for gunplay didn't diminish his popularity. Many cowboys still considered him a kindly father-figure. John Muarry, the would-be peacemaker, recuperated at Mulhall's home after his release from the Emergency Hospital. Will Rogers remained loyal to the Colonel. In a letter to his father he wrote, "They can say what they please about Mulhall but he has done more for us boys than any man on earth."

For appearances sake, the exposition's directors banned Mulhall from the fairgrounds. Then The Pike's wild west concession ran into even more problems. Those Sunday performances created a conflict with the exposition's directors. The St. Louis Humane Society declared that steer-roping exhibitions constituted cruelty to animals. In September, Cummins was fired as the concession's manager, and replaced by Captain Visser of the Boer War exhibit. The show's employees went on strike in support of Cummins.

Will briefly cast his lot with another western show in St. Louis. It was run by a San Antonio, Texan named Charles Tomkins. During that stint, he had his own run in with the St. Louis police. A minor beef with a patrolman at a trolley stop earned him a paddy wagon ride. He spent that night in jail and was released the next afternoon.

Zach Mulhall's career as an impresario was far from over. He started staging shows every Sunday at 3 p.m. at the Delmar Race Track. Will quickly rejoined his old friend. The Colonel billed him as "the most expert fancy roper in America."

That show often drew crowds of over 10,000. Mulhall had wisely added a glittering geriatric star to his roster.

On June 6, Geronimo had arrived at the World's Fair in the custody of U. S. Army Captain S. Sayre. Geronimo was at least 75 years old and a military prisoner at Fort Sill, Oklahoma.

That didn't prevent government authorities from allowing him to be exhibited at special events throughout the country. In 1898, he became a major attraction at the Trans-Pacific Exposition in Omaha. The promoters of Buffalo's 1901 Pan-American Exposition paid $45 a month for his services.

Geronimo resided in his own teepee at the Louisiana Purchase Exposition's Apache Village. He immediately became one of the exposition's most acclaimed celebrities.

The elderly chieftain recalled in his published memoirs, "Many people in St. Louis invited me to come to their homes, but my keepers always refused. Every Sunday the President of the Fair sent for me to go to a wild west show. I took part in the roping contests. There were many other Indian tribes there, and strange people of whom I have never met."

In spite of his age and rheumatism, Geronimo more than held his own in roping competitions. On several occasions, he was pitted against the formidable Lucille Mulhall.

This was no ordinary wild west show. One Sunday, Mulhall had

African pygmies from the Fair's anthropological exhibit stage a war dance. He rewarded them with an enormous watermelon, and they delighted the audience by devouring it on the spot. On July 31, Theodore Roosevelt Jr. and his little brother Kermit were among the cheering spectators.

Will worked up the courage to make his vaudeville debut in St. Louis. During his South African sojourn, Texas Jack had suggested that his rope tricks would be a hit with vaudeville audiences.

Will premiered his stage act at the Standard Theater. Its manager wrote, "I take great pleasure in recommending Will Rogers in his specialty. I played him at the Standard Theater, and he proved a decided novelty. He will make good on any bill, and can follow any headliner."

Will parlayed that testimonial into a $30 offer for a one week engagement at Chicago's Opera House. At first, he was categorized as a dumb act. That was vaudeville's term for performers who could dazzle audiences for 10-12 minutes with a visual specialty that didn't require verbal accompaniment.

Will's unique specialty and western costume made him a very bookable entertainer. He sensed that he had bright vaudeville prospects, and devised an improvement to his act.

Rogers decided to demonstrate many different roping techniques by lassoing a horse on stage. Mulhall owned a dark bay pony with a black mane and tail. The Colonel named it Teddy, in honor of the President. A man would ride Teddy across the stage several times. On each ride, Will used a different technique to rope them. This act required an intelligent horse that could maneuver on a small indoor stage. Teddy fit the bill.

• • • • • • • • • • • • • •
Louisiana Purchase Exposition President David R. Francis presented him with a first prize blue ribbon for his roping performance.
• • • • • • • • • • • • • •

Will's success at the Chicago Opera House didn't keep him from St. Louis for long. St. Louis remained his base throughout the run of the World's Fair. He continued performing in Zach Mulhall's racetrack production, and participating in official exposition events.

On November 12, 1904, he was one of 50 cowhands in the free wild west exhibition that closed the World's Fair Southern Breeding and Cattle Range Show. That extravaganza took place in the exposition's

Livestock Forum.

Louisiana Purchase Exposition President David R. Francis presented him with a first-prize blue ribbon for his roping performance. Rogers would later admit, "I am kinder foolish about my little ribbon."

All was going well for him in September of 1904. He was pleasantly surprised to get Betty Blake's letter. Five minutes after reading it, he replied with a friendly invitation to his Sunday performance at the Delmar Race Track.

Betty, her sister and a friend attended together. He tried to impress Betty by wearing the gold-braided red velvet suit he had sported in Australia. Betty would recall later, "He looked so funny. ... I was so embarrassed when my sister and Mary gave me sidelong looks and smiled at the costume."

Will fared better with her when that show was over. Somehow, he lured Betty away from her companions. He took her to the Irish Pavilion on The Pike where they enjoyed John McCormack's exquisite tenor voice. McCormack would become one of his closest show business friends.

Will and Betty made a date for the next day. He had to cancel it to go to Claremore, Oklahoma and pick up a horse. Fortunately, Will had enough sense to send Betty an apologetic note.

This young lady apparently understood a cowboy's priorities. She wrote him back. Their correspondence continued after she returned to Rogers, Arkansas. They would always remember their date at the St. Louis World's Fair.

Will continued to reside with the Mulhall's throughout the run of the Louisiana Purchase Exposition. In January of 1905, a St. Louis court found Zach Mulhall guilty of assault with intent to kill and sentenced him to three years in prison. The Colonel successfully appealed that verdict and never served jail time.

That April, Will joined Mulhall for a triumphant east coast tour that included a White House performance. The Washington Times lauded Will as "perhaps the finest rope man in the world."

Will and his equine partner, Teddy, continued to improve their vaudeville act. They worked their way up to headlining theaters throughout America.

That affable Oklahoman continued to write and visit the woman who reentered his life at the St. Louis World's Fair. He proposed marriage to her on many occasions. Convincing Betty Blake to become a showman's wife would take time, because she was a very practical young woman.

By 1908, Will was steadily earning $250 a week on the vaudeville circuit. Betty was finally convinced that he could provide for a family.

On November 25 of that year, they tied the knot in Rogers, Arkansas. They spent the first day of their honeymoon in St. Louis. Will later wrote, "The day I roped Betty, I did the star performance of my life."

That performance might never have occurred if it hadn't been for the good fortune that reunited them in St. Louis. Betty Blake was a properly brought up young woman. Dispatching that note to Will was a brazen act by 1904 society's standards.

Betty later admitted, "Though I wanted to see Will very much, I had a wide streak of conventionality in me." Perhaps the cosmopolitan atmosphere of that enormous World's Fair encouraged that country girl to boldly take a chance at romance.

The Louisiana Purchase Exposition's turnstiles recorded nearly twenty million admissions from April 30 through December 1, 1904. Will and Betty Rogers were probably not the only couple that began or renewed a romance there.

Will Rogers had many reasons to remember his St. Louis sojourn. The Standard Theater gave him his vaudeville debut. Teddy became his long-time stage partner. The horse he acquired from Zach Mulhall died peacefully in 1917.

Will saw the Colonel for the last time in 1931. Walt Harrison, who witnessed Will's final meeting with the 84 year old Mulhall, wrote, "He was crying like a baby as he put his arms around Will, and the tears in Rogers' eyes were not caused by the biting wind that was blowing. ... I saw Will hug the old boy like a mother hugs her baby. Then, he whispered in his ear, and stuck a roll of bills that would choke a horse into the old man's hand."

Will and Betty remained happily married until his tragic death in a plane crash on August 15, 1935. They always treasured memories of hearing John McCormack sing at the Irish Pavilion on that Sunday evening in 1904. Will and Betty Rogers truly had a date with destiny at the St. Louis World's Fair. ❖

The Jefferson Arms

A writer in the June 1903 *World's Fair Bulletin* promised, "the city will not be found wanting in preparations to fittingly entertain the stranger from the uttermost parts." The 40-room Jefferson was the grandest of the dozen new hotels that fulfilled his promise.

The Hotel Jefferson Corporation was formed on May 19, 1903. A.B. Gaines, D.F. Platt, Festus J. Wade, Lyman T. Hay, Sam W. Fordyce, Lorenzo Anderson, and Jacob Klein, were the original stockholders. Hay served as the first general manager.

• • • • • • • • • • • •
The hotel's life would continue long after the World's Fair closed.
• • • • • • • • • • • •

Mr. and Mrs. Dan C. Nugent of St. Louis were the first guests to sign the registry when the hotel opened on May 1, 1904 (the day after the Fair opened). Mr. Nugent remarked, "If all the guests are as well accommodated as the party I entertained at dinner, this hotel will never want for patronage."

That evening, the hotel devoted three floors to a grand ball given by the local chapter of the Daughters of the Confederacy. Mayor and Mrs. Rolla Wells and Governor and Mrs. David Francis were among the dignitaries who greeted guests.

The ballroom was lavishly decorated with the flags of nations that had sent commissioners to the Fair. An international assembly of courtly gentlemen and ladies waltzed in formal attire. Miss Sartorius, granddaughter of President U.S. Grant, was among the belles of the ball.

The hotel's life would continue long after the Fair closed on December 1, 1904. Located in the heart of the downtown entertainment district, it became a Mecca for socialites.

In 1916, Lilburn A. Kingsbury wrote of a typical night at

FIVE HUNDRED MEN WORKING ON JEFFERSON HOTEL.

A newspaper photo and article from the September 1, 1903 edition of The Republic shows, according to the caption, the "present state of construction of the Hotel Jefferson". The accompanying articles states that the brick walls of the hotel "will probably be completed by Wednesday" and that "plasterers will begin work on the walls and ceilings next week." The article goes on to say, "In order to turn the building over to the owners on February 1, the contractors are rushing the work, employing their artisans eleven hours a day. Five hundred men are working on the Structure." (Front the collections of Max Storm.)

Present stage of construction of the Hotel Jefferson, at Twelfth and Locust streets.

The brick walls of the new Jefferson Hotel, which is being built at the corner of Twelfth and Locust streets, will probably be completed by Wednesday, The scaffolding will be torn down Thursday.

The electric wiring and gas fittings for the first ten floors are in and wires and gas fittings are being placed in the eleventh and twelfth floors.

Plumbers are also putting in sewer and water connections throughout the building.

Plasterers will begin work on the walls and ceilings next week.

The Jefferson Hotel is being built at a cost of $1,000,000 by a stock company formed by the Mercantile Trust Company. The work is being done by the Westlake Construction Company. In order to turn the building over to the owners on February 1, the contractors are rushing the work, employing their artisans eleven hours a day. Five hundred men are working on the structure.

In building the walls, 2,000,000 bricks were used. To erect the steel work, 100,000 tons of metal were used. Each girder on the first floor weighs about thirty-six tons.

the Jefferson, "…Dozens of limousines unload gladrags full of humanity who want to eat and drink after the theaters … the guests can dance between courses … they have a lovely time."

Many of them sipped the concoctions of bartender Nick Fricke. A young Greek immigrant named Charles P. Skouras was Fricke's assistant. Skouras later became president of National Theaters Corporation.

Diners savored specialties like pig's knuckles and sauerkraut, potato dumplings, and steak tartare prepared by Chef Otto Klopfer, the 350-lb. culinary craftsman who had been Kaiser Wilhelm II's private chef aboard the imperial yacht, The Hohenzollern.

The elegant dining facilities – including the Gold, Crystal and Ivory Rooms – could accommodate up to 2,000 guest simultaneously. The staff, consisting of 20 cooks, 10 pantry women, two stewards, 125 waiters, four captains, two food checkers, and scores of dish, pan, and pot washers was constantly busy. An average of 3,000 pieces of silverware were polished each day.

The Gold Room was the annual scene of the Queen's supper following the Veiled Prophet Ball. Margaret Truman was the toast of that event in 1947.

Over 100 major conventions convened at the Jefferson in a typical year. It was Woodrow Wilson's headquarters when St. Louis hosted the Democratic party's national convention in 1916. Delegates to the American Legion's first national convention filled the rooms in 1935.

Mary Pickford, Helen Traubel, Arthur Rubinstein, Lauritz Melchoir, Alben B. Barkley, Harry S. Truman, John L. Lewis, Robert A. Taft, and Enrico Caruso were among the scores of celebrities who signed the guest registry over the years. Caruso reportedly offered one of the doormen a job as his personal valet.

National and local entertainers performed in the hotel's Boulevard Room. St. Louisan, Virginia Mayo, catapulted from its chorus line to Hollywood stardom in the 1940s.

The Jefferson underwent many management changes during its 71 years as a transient inn. In 1927, Max Teich and Carl C. Roessler purchased controlling interest and spent over $2,000,000 on expanding its size to 800 rooms.

The Hilton Hotel Corporation bought the building for $4,000,000 in 1950, and spent another $2,200,000 on improvements like a 24-hour drugstore, and three dining rooms: The Tudor, The Town, and The Minute Chef. During the first half of the 50s, the Jefferson was a link in the international chain that included the Waldorf Astoria and Roosevelt Hotels in New York, the Palmer House in Chicago and the Mayflower in Washington D.C.

Anti-trust action forced Hilton to sell the Jefferson to the Sheraton Corporation of America for $ 7,500,000 in 1955. They changed the name to the Sheraton-Jefferson, and spent an additional $350,000 on modernization. The Sheraton-Jefferson became St. Louis' first fully-air conditioned hotel.

The city's downtown convention trade dwindled during the 1960s. Sheraton executives questioned the profitability of an aging downtown property. The Sheraton Hotel chain, including the Sheraton-Jefferson, was sold to a wholly-owned subsidiary of the International Telephone and Telegraph Company in 1968.

White Holdings Ltd. acquired the hotel in 1973. Edward D. Gales, a St. Louis real estate investor, bought it from them in 1975. He terminated its eventful life as a transient hotel on July 23, 1975.

The Jefferson Arms retirement community opened two years later. Many of the residents are life-long St. Louisans who witnessed historic moments at the Jefferson Hotel. Some recall the first meeting of the National Monuments Commission in the Adolphus Room in 1934. The efforts of the committee, chaired by Senator Alben B. Barkley of Kentucky, eventually led to the building of the Gateway Arch.

Many were in the Gold Room when Admiral Halsey launched the Victory Bond drive in October 1945. Others treasure memories of shaking hands with Harry and Bess Truman in the lobby.

Venerable baseball fans reminisce about the many Cardinals and Browns who touched base at the Jefferson. Jocko Conlan, a famous umpire, said in the 1960s, "this hotel makes you feel at home … guys come in just to talk baseball."

Opera buffs treasure memories of seeing Traubel and Melchoir snacking in the coffee shop. Russ David and his Orchestra were perennial hits in the Boulevard Room.

During the Hilton ownership, each room contained an anthology of short stories personally selected by Conrad Hilton. Jefferson Arms residents feel that the most exciting chapter in the history of a building that was originally built to accomodate visitors to the Fair, is still being written.

The Jefferson Arms is once again "a city within the city" that laid out the red carpet for the world in 1904. The spirit of the St. Louis World's Fair lives at the Jefferson Arms. ⚜

A Model Thanksgiving

On November 24, 1904, three-hundred and twenty-six children of all nations enjoyed their first American Thanksgiving dinner in a place that no longer exists. That place was the Great Pavilion of the Model Playground at the Louisiana Purchase Exposition.

Those youngsters lived in different tribal villages within the Fairgrounds. They were part of what a 1904 commentator called, "the concourse of strange peoples, such as one would not be able to see in an ordinary journey around the earth. ... Never before have so many tribes been brought together as may be seen at the World's Fair."

Mr. Betts and Mrs. Hirschfield wanted the children of all nationalities to experience a real American Thanksgiving celebration.

The Model Playground was located on the Model Street. That 1,200 foot long boulevard occupied the northeastern corner of the Fairgrounds. All of its public buildings, street lamps, fire plugs, lamp posts, and street fixtures, exemplified the highest achievements in urban design. A journalist lauded it as, " a materialization in buildings, parks, and driveways of the beautiful theories of social economy."

That exhibit's coordinators had expected visitors to marvel at their Model Town Hall, Hospital, and Museum. They were amazed when the Model Playground became their most noted attraction.

That remarkable facility was

"Mrs. Hirschfield comforts a child of the Orient." ("World's Fair Bulletin", September 1904, World's Fair Publishing Company. From the collection of Ron Schira.)

designed and directed by Mrs. Ruth Ashley Hirschfield of New York City. She earned a degree from New York University and became one of the few female members of the New York State bar. She received funding for her project from the exposition's Board of Lady Governors and Joseph See of Boston, Massachusetts. Mr. See had provided Boston with the money to build its renowned Columbus Avenue playgrounds.

Mrs. Hirschfield had exhibited her acclaimed Model Household Nursery at the 1901 Pan-American Exposition in Buffalo, New York. She presented a more elaborate version of that exhibit in the Palace of Education at the 1904 World's Fair.

Mrs. Hirschfield had long crusaded for the establishment of playgrounds and child care programs. She designed her World's Fair playground to serve as an example for all communities. The Social and Economic Jury of the Louisiana Purchase Exposition awarded it a grand prize.

She planned a child's dreamland of spacious pavilions, canopies, cottages, outdoor croquet and basketball courts, and restrooms equipped with tubs and showers. It's outdoor gymnasium had enough parallel bars, ladders, springboards, swings, see-saws, tumbling mats, and trapezes to delight 600 fledgling acrobats at one time.

The nursery provided a full day of care for infants as young as two weeks. The kindergarten building was well stocked with musical instruments, educational toys, and books. Children up to age 14 participated in physical education classes. Cooks prepared two meals a day in the dietary kitchen. Children with special nutritional needs were accommodated. Sleepyheads napped in a special pavilion containing hundreds of hammocks and mattresses.

Twelve nurses were among Mrs. Hirschfield's 22 assistants. Many parents who worked at the Exposition checked their children in each morning and returned for them in the late after-

"Little Rosie, the favorite of the Orient, Playing 'At the Sea Shore' at Model Playground." ("World's Fair Bulletin", September 1904, World's Fair Publishing Company. From the collection of Ron Schira.)

A Model Thanksgiving

noon. Thousands of World's Fair visitors also enrolled their children in this pioneer day care program. The Model Playground offered this service six days a week. Parents gladly paid a nominal fee. Over 1,200 needy children received care, free of charge.

During its 165 day history, that playground opened its gates to 20,911 children not enrolled in the day care program. Adult fairgoers often paused to watch through the surrounding wire fence. In that era, many American youngsters had to get a job by the age of 11. Adults rejoiced in seeing children at play.

No previous World's Fair had offered such a facility. Respected physicians called it a therapeutic environment for frail children. Mrs. Hirschfield generously opened her dreamland to local schools and orphanages. School groups of deaf and blind children became her fr quent guests.

The Louisiana Purchase Exposition was the first World's Fair to have a Lost Children's Bureau. The Model Playground provided free care to a total of 1,166 lost little ones. All of them were safely reunited with their parents.

No accidents ever took place on the Model Playground. No child ever became ill there. That peaceful play environment was never disrupted by any form of violence.

Parents highly praised the treatment their children received from Mrs. Hirschfield and her staff. Many toddlers wept when they said goodbye to their care providers.

On Sunday afternoons, that playground hosted the Congress of All Nationalities. Eskimo tots frolicked in the sand-box. Asian and Native American children faced one another on see-saws. African Pygmy and Kaffir children mastered croquet. Young people from around the world joined in harmonious child's play.

They became featured players in many of the Model Playground's grandest events. A gala party was held in their honor on June 14. On July 31, they met President Theodore Roosevelt's sons and the Foreign, National, and State Commissioners of the Louisiana Purchase Exposition.

August 2 was the first Children's Day at the St. Louis World's Fair. The children of all nationalities met at the Model Playground and lined up for a gala parade. They wore their native clothing while riding on everything from elephants to Eskimo sleds.

On September 15, they gathered there to meet the members and delegates of the Interparlimentary Peace Union. On November 2, Miss Helen Miller Gould paid them a visit. That philanthropist was renowned for her efforts on behalf of mothers and children. Many admiring adults crowded around the playground fence to

"Boys enjoying themselves at the Gymnasium at the Model Playground." ("World's Fair Bulletin", September 1904, World's Fair Publishing Company. From the collection of Ron Schira.)

doff their caps in her honor. At the end of the day, she placed a toy in the hands of each child.

Mr. Frederick A. Betts of Hartford, Connecticut was a member of the National Commission to the World's Fair, and one of the playground's greatest admirers. He choose to celebrate his birthday there. That day, August 8, happened to be another Children's Day at the Fair. He and his wife treated 1,600 kids to ice cream, birthday cake, and maple sugar. His grateful guests unanimously proclaimed Mr. Betts and the Model Playground the real thing.

Mr. Betts and Mrs. Hirschfield wanted the children of all nationalities to experience a real American Thanksgiving celebration. Many prominent St. Louisans helped them prepare an extraordinary event.

On November 24, William Weil and his World's Fair band led those jubilant children into the Great Pavilion. They were seated at 29 beautifully decorated tables. Local businesses had donated everything from celery to chocolate. This was truly a magnificent feast. Reverend Columbus Polk Goodson of the Kingshighway Cumberland Presbyterian Church delivered the blessing. St. Louis Postmaster, Frank Wyman, led the singing of the Doxology.

Then Mrs. Hirschfield signaled her many adult helpers to begin serving heaping platters of turkey and cranberry sauce. Some of St. Louis' most illustrious socialites gladly obeyed her command.

While the children enjoyed their first American Thanksgiving fare, St. Louis Mayor, Rolla Wells, and Louisiana Purchase Exposition

A Model Thanksgiving

President, David R. Francis, spoke about the meaning of the holiday. Then the youngsters called on Mr. Betts to speak. His response was simply, "welcome to all and God bless you, may you heartily enjoy yourselves." All 326 children gave Mr. Betts and Mrs. Hirschfield a standing ovation.

After their banquet, the children lined up to receive a bag of sweets from the Blanke-Wennecker Candy Company and a toy from Mrs. J.H. Vaill. The World's Fair band played *The Star Spangled Banner*. The youngsters returned to their villages at the exposition. Three hundred adults had worked to give those children an unforgettable Thanksgiving. Twenty thousand admiring fairgoers had watched through the playground fence.

The Louisiana Purchase Exposition ended at midnight on December 1, 1904. It would serve as a model for future World's Fairs.

Only that truly international exposition could have brought the children of all nations together. The Model Playground enabled thousands of adults to see them at play.

Every exhibit on the Model Street represented the fulfillment of beautiful social theories. The Model Playground quickly became its most acclaimed attraction. It helped thousands of adults see that children playing in peace exemplify the highest hope of civilization.

David R. Francis speaking to children at the Model Playground. ("History of the Louisiana Purchase Exposition", Universal Exposition Publishing Company, 1905. From the collection of Ron Schira.)

They learned that truly civilized people care about the welfare of all children. Mrs. Ruth Ashley Hirschfield's creation inspired many public playgrounds and child care programs.

In 1621, the members of the Plymouth Bay colony invited their Native American neighbors to a great feast of Thanksgiving. The traditional American Thanksgiving banquet is the legacy of that celebration. The participants in the Thanksgiving celebration at the 1904 Louisiana Purchase Exposition created their own legacy. All of those adults and children were, indeed, the real thing. The highest hope of civilization was realized in the example they gave the world at the Model Playground. ⚜

The Typical American

The typical American arrived at the St. Louis World's Fair on Saturday, November 26, 1904. His name was Theodore Roosevelt. This was the eagerly awaited President's Day.

The three-coach railroad train bearing the President, Mrs. Roosevelt, and their daughter Alice was parked on tracks west of the Palace of Transportation at 4 a.m. A formidable line of Jefferson Guards and St. Louis policemen was immediately posted around it.

• • • • • • • • • • • • • • •

The Louisiana Purchase Exposition opened on April 30, 1904. It was internationally acclaimed as the coronation of civilization.

• • • • • • • • • • • • • • • •

David R. Francis, President of the Louisiana Purchase Exposition, led a procession from the Administration Building to the President's train at 9 a.m. Mayor Rolla Wells, Corwin H. Spencer, F.D. Hirschberg, and C.P. Walbridge were among the local dignitaries who would accompany the Roosevelts on their Exposition tour.

The President had dedicated the Exposition's buildings on April 30, 1903. He appeared with former President Grover Cleveland on that occasion to commemorate the 100th anniversary of the signing of the Louisiana Purchase Treaty. Roosevelt was so impressed by the ceremonial pageantry that he choose to forego lunch rather than abandon the reviewing stand. Dedication Week ended on Saturday, May 2, 1903. St. Louis prepared to host the millions that would flock to the Fair in 1904.

A writer in the June 1903 issue of *The World's Fair Bulletin* made this promise on behalf of the nation's fourth largest city:

"... The World's Fair of 1904 is accepted in all the words imply. It carries with it obligations. Much will be expected of the state to which much has been given ... 'The duty of St. Louis' has come into sudden and national attention... It is no longer necessary to prove that this is to be a World's Fair. The world admits it and welcomes it. But the world, through its mouth-pieces, the newspapers, rises to comment upon the shortcomings of dedication, to utter warnings against overcharges and to advise what a city with a World's Fair on its hands owes to the world. The World's Fair is not for St. Louis, but by St. Louis for the world ...

"On the thirtieth of April, 1904, there will be rooms with baths for all, quick transit and cosmopolitan manners everywhere... The community which has created the physical part of a World's Fair in a manner to challenge world-wide admiration and unstinted commendation, will not be found wanting in preparations to fittingly entertain the stranger from the uttermost parts ... The pride of a city which is equal to the physical creation of the World's Fair will not suffer the presence of a fly in the ointment."

The Louisiana Purchase Exposition officially opened on April 30, 1904. It was internationally acclaimed as the "coronation of civilization." St. Louisans were eager for Roosevelt to see how splendidly they had done their duty. William H. Thompson, the Treasurer of the Louisiana Purchase Exposition, made a special trip to the White House in July of 1904. Thompson, Roosevelt's trusted friend and political ally, urged him to visit the Exposition.

Roosevelt had been elected Vice-President on William McKinley's ticket in 1900. McKinley was shot by Leon Czolgosz on the steps of the Music Hall at the Buffalo Exposition on September 6, 1901. Eight days later, McKinley died at the home of the Buffalo

President Theodore Roosevelt, David R. Francis, and others participate in President's Day festivities. (From a stereo view by Underwood & Underwood. From the collection of Yvonne Suess.

The Typical American

Exposition's director. Roosevelt became the nation's 26th President.

The Republican Party selected him as their presidential candidate in 1904. The President didn't want to give the impression of exploiting the Fair for political purposes. He assured Thompson that he planned to visit St. Louis after Election Day.

On Tuesday, November 2, Roosevelt received an overwhelming mandate from the American people. David R. Francis read this disappointing letter to the Exposition's Executive Committee at its meeting on November 8:

The White House
Washington, D.C.

November 5, 1904

My Dear Governor Francis,

I am sorry to say that it begins to look more and more as if it would be a sheer impossibility for me to get out to the World's Fair. Naturally, I have not been able to do much work on my message (to Congress) as yet. There will be but three weeks between the election and the meeting of Congress. During these three weeks there are two functions of international character here at Washington, and I am afraid that it is an absolute impossibility for me to fulfill these official duties here and go to the Fair. I cannot say how disappointed I am not to be able to attend the exposition. I have been hoping against hope that I should be able to go, and had arranged with Senator Fairbanks to go together.

Permit me to express to you most warmly my appreciation of what you have done. You have had a very hard task, and you have had my warmest sympathy all through it, and you have done it admirably.

With high regard, believe me,

Sincerely yours,

Theodore Roosevelt

Francis wouldn't take no for an answer. He asked his friend, Navy Secretary Paul Morton, to urge the President to reconsider. Thompson paid another call on his friend in the White House. They somehow managed to change Roosevelt's mind. President's Day was hastily set for November 26, the Saturday after Thanksgiving.

This was a truly elegant occasion. Shortly after 9 a.m., the presidential party left their train in stately carriages. The Secret Service men who walked beside the President's carriage sported top hats and frock coats. Over 200,000 fairgoers cheered the presidential party.

The Palace of Liberal Arts and the Government Building were the first stops on the Roosevelts itinerary. From his reviewing stand in front of the Palace of Manufacturers, the Commander-in-Chief witnessed a 2,000-man military parade.

Then the Roosevelts toured the pavilions of Germany, France, Mexico, Great Britain, Holland, Sweden, Austria, Belgium, China, Cuba, Brazil, Italy, and Japan. The First Family was showered with gifts. The President received an 800 year old painting at the Chinese Pavilion. The Italian government's representative presented Mrs. Roosevelt with a bronze statue of the Dancing Faun.

The Roosevelts lunched at the restaurant in the West Pavilion. At 3:00 p.m., they watched the kickoff of the Carlisle-Haskell football game at the World's Fair Stadium. The teams represented the U.S. Government Indian Schools in Carlisle, Pennsylvania and Lawrence, Kansas. The official game program stated: "Both teams are made up of seasoned players, all full-blooded Indians."

The Roosevelts spent several hours at the Philippine Exhibit. Miss Pilar Zamora's Igorote students serenaded them with My Country Tis of Thee at the Philippine Model School. The President exclaimed, "it is wonderful, such advancement and in so short a time!"

The First Family received an unusual gift at one of the Moro Villages. Datto Facunda, an elderly warrior, professed to have no further use for the bolo he had used to kill three enemies. He graciously surrendered it to the President.

The Cascades was the scene of a spectacular sundown fireworks display. Then the Roosevelts watched from the Palace of Electricity as the entire Exposition was electrically illuminated in their honor.

The Roosevelts enjoyed a one hour rest at William H. Thompson's Lindell Boulevard mansion before attending a grand banquet at the

Tyrolean Alps. Governor LaFollette of Wisconsin, Governor A.M. Dockery of Missouri, and Governor VanSant of Minnesota were among the 600 guests.

The dishes on the lavish menu honored the President's passion for hunting, his New York home and his Exposition visit – Quail Hunter Style, Salad Oyster Bay, and Medallions of Beef Louisiana.

Reverend Daniel S. Tuttle of the Episcopal Diocese of Missouri delivered the invocation. Then David R. Francis said in proposing a toast:

> "This is a red-letter day at the World's Fair, the greatest exposition of all times. ... The work of this Exposition began six and one-half years ago. ... Seven months ago this Exposition was opened. All promises made have been fulfilled. Still the Exposition would have been incomplete, there would have been an aching void that could not have been filled, if we had not been honored by the presence of the President of the United States.
>
> "The Chief Executive of the American Republic not only represents the sovereignty of 80,000,000 people, but after election as President he stands for the spirit of the people.
>
> "He is the typical American. He personifies the highest motives, and the best instincts and ambitions of a free people. As this Exposition is drawing to a close a fitting climax is the presence of one who is not only the President of the United States but the President-elect as well. He is the emphatic choice of the American people."

After Francis received a thunderous ovation, the typical American delivered this address:

> "I count it, indeed, a privilege to have had a chance of visiting this marvelous Exposition. I cannot sufficiently express my appreciation of its wonder and its beauty. It is in very fact, the greatest Exposition of the kind that we have ever seen in recorded history.
>
> "As I walked today through and among the buildings and saw what they were and what they contained, what they signified in the way of achievement at home, what they signified in the way of achievement among these great and friendly nations who are represented here, I had but one regret, and that was a deep regret – the regret that these could not be made permanent.
>
> "The regret is that it is impossible to keep these buildings as they are for our children and our children's children and all who are to come after as our permanent memorial of the greatness of this country.
>
> "I think that the American who grudges a dollar that he has

spent here is not so farsighted as he should be.

"It is a credit to the United States that this Exposition should have been carried to so successful a conclusion; and, of course, it is preeminitely a credit to Missouri and to St. Louis ... on behalf of the people of the nation, I wish to express my deep appreciation of the farsighted, tireless, intelligent, work that has been done by all who are responsible for this Exposition, and, more than by all others, by you, President Francis.

"The country is under a great debt of obligation to you and your associates, and I am glad of this opportunity to express, however imperfectly, my sense of this obligation ..."

A brief concert by Karl Komzak's 100-piece Exposition Orchestra ended the banquet. The Roosevelts embarked on a carriage tour of the State buildings in the Plateau of States at 9:00 p.m. It was nearly midnight before those weary tourists retired to their Pullman car.

> **The typical American declared, "Why, my boy, I've had the time of my life!"**

The Roosevelts remained in St. Louis on Sunday, November 27. After attending church in the morning, they enjoyed an afternoon carriage ride and leisurely visits at the homes of Thompson and Francis.

The presidential party departed St. Louis at 12:01 a.m. on Monday to avoid traveling on the Sabbath. As the train started moving, the leader of 80,000,000 people stepped out on the back platform and gazed upon the shadowy outlines of the Exposition buildings. Then he turned back in to the car, where an Eastern newspaper corespondent asked him how he had enjoyed his visit. The typical American declared, "Why, my boy, I've had the time of my life!" ⚜

A Christmas Carol Named St. Louis

Even on the muggiest summer afternoons, seeing the magnificent statue of Louis IX, the 13th-century French king, makes me thing about Christmas. The equestrian statue of the crusader king graces the front entrance of the city's Art Museum in Forest Park. It was originally a plaster statue in a plaza at the 1904 St. Louis World's Fair. When the exposition was over, it was recast in bronze and moved to the top of Art Hill, where it has become a symbol of civic pride and a local landmark.

• • • • • • • • • • • •

One of the world's most beloved Christmas carols was originally titled St. Louis.

• • • • • • • • • • • •

Louis IX was the patron saint of Louis XV, the reigning French monarch when the city was founded on February 14, 1764. The settlement was first called Laclede's Village. A Jesuit priest, the Rev. Sebastian Meurin, had established the first church in the area and called it, "The Mission of St. Louis to the Illinois Indians." The entire settlement took on the name of the church.

In the stately bronze on Art Hill, the saint holds his sword high in the air with the hilt up to form the Cross. In this gesture, we see a gentle warrior turning a weapon of battle into a symbol of peace. And that's why the statue always reminds me of the birth of the prince of peace — that and the fact that one of the world's most beloved Christmas carols was originally titled St. Louis. It has since become far better known by the name, O *Little Town of Bethlehem*.

The Rev. Phillip Brooks was pastor at an Episcopal church in Philadelphia when the American Civil War ended in April 1865. Later that year, he traveled to the holy land and rode on horseback from Jerusalem to Bethlehem on Christmas Eve. He experienced the joy of standing in the Field of the Shepherd at twilight and worshipping in the five-hour service at the Church of the Nativity.

Three years later, he wrote a lovely five-stanza poem to express the way he had felt on the evening in the holy land. He asked Lewis Redner, his church organist, to set his verses to music. Brooks hoped that Redner would be

Louis the IX, the Crusader King, was located near the entrance to the Fair on the Plaza of St. Louis. During the Fair, the sculpture was made of staff, the same "temporary material" that was used in the construction of all the statues and the main palaces of the fairgrounds. Some time after the Fair, the statue was recast in bronze, and placed in its present location at the top of Art Hill. (From a stereo view by Keystone View Company. From the collection of Yvonne Suess.)

inspired to turn his poem into a song that the Sunday school children of their church could sing for people of all ages. He had very little time before the Sunday service on December 27, 1868, in which to accomplish this difficult task. The pastor realized this and jokingly promised that if Redner responded to the challenge with an exceptionally fine tune, he would name their musical creation "St. Lewis".

From the moment those Philadelphia Sunday school children performed it to the present day, the carol has reminded people of the feeling of peace and good will toward all that came into the world when Christ was born. The delighted Rev. Brooks kept the promise he made, but to avoid embarrassing the modest church organist, he changed the spelling of Redner's first name. The song first appeared in the Episcopal hymnal in 1892 as St. Louis. People so vividly remembered the words of its first line that the carol would eventually become better known as *O Little Town of Bethlehem*.

A Christmas Carol Named St. Louis

I love climbing up Art Hill and seeing the bronze figure of the mounted crusader. The statue and the museum were both created for the 1904 World's Fair that brought people from all over the world to the city I call home. I think of all the people who came to St. Louis for that fair and all the people who have journeyed to the birthplace of Christ in Bethlehem. I think of the Rev. Brooks and Lewis Redner creating a musical message of peace and good will that would first be voiced by children in their Philadelphia Sunday school. I recall one of the favorite mottos of good King St. Louis, "I have fought a good fight, I have kept the faith."

I tremble with joy whenever I behold the statue of the noble crusader raising the holy cross high in the air. Thoughts of the gentle St. Louis and the beautiful Christmas carol inspired by a visit to Bethlehem inspire me to keep the faith that, one day, we will live in a world where all weapons of war will be turned into symbols of peace. I feel with all of my heart that this faith is truly the spirit of St. Louis, the spirit of Bethlehem and the spirit of Christmas. ⚜

"It is sweet recollection –

the days of 1904!

Their memory

lightens our cares,

broadens our vision,

rejuvenates our hearts.

May it never grow dim!"

David R. Francis
President
Louisiana Purchase Exposition Co.
December 1, 1904

About Bert Minkin

Bert Minkin was a St. Louis author, lecturer, and historian, whose articles and stories have appeared in such newspapers and periodicals as "The St. Louis Post-Dispatch," "The St. Louis Jewish Light," "The Lutheran Witness," "Lutheran Digest," "A New Day," and "The Annals of St. Anne Beaupre."

Minkin's "A Word With You" column was a regular feature in "Senior Circuit." He was a feature writer for "The Webster-Kirkwood Times" and "The South County Times."

Minkin was the author of such books as *Lenten Meditations* (Lutheran Hour Ministries, 1996) and *Storytelling Recipes for Christian Teachers* (Concordia Publishing House, 1996). Minkin gave over 5,000 public lectures and story performances for such sponsors as the Missouri Historical Society, Harvard Divinity School, Northwestern University, the Missouri Botanical Garden, Phillips Andover Academy, Stanford University, and the University of Chicago.

Minkin received his B.A. from Beloit College and M.A. from the University of California Berkeley. He was an English teacher at Phillips Brooks School in North Andover, MA, and an artist-in-residence for such prep schools an Northfield-Mt. Hermon, Choate-Rosemary Hall, Groton, the Gunnery, and Hotchkiss School.

He also taught numerous classes for OASIS, the Thomas Dunn Memorials, the Writers' Voice, and the Missouri Alliance for Arts Education. He was a featured scholar/lecturer for the American Mirror Speaker's Bureau of the Missouri Humanities Council since 1994.

Learn More About the 1904 World's Fair Society

In April 1986, a handful of people got together to discuss the formation of a society dedicated to preserving the memories and memorabilia of the Louisiana Purchase Exposition. On April 30, 1986, the 82nd anniversary of the opening day of the Fair, we held our first official membership meeting. We started small, but we were a determined bunch… with our membership growing to over 500 as we prepared to celebrate the centennial of the Fair in 2004.

We are a diverse group of people. Some of us are collectors … some of us are interested in digging up the facts and setting the record straight … some of us are interested in finding the bits and pieces that still exist … some of us actually attended the Fair and enjoy sharing our memories.

In 1904, St. Louis recognized the importance of the Louisiana Purchase Treaty to the history of the United States, by inviting the country and the world to participate in the "greatest of expositions." *The 1904 World's Fair Society wants to keep those memories alive.*

www.1904worldsfairsociety.org